HOW TO TRY A
MURDER

THE HANDBOOK FOR
ARMCHAIR LAWYERS

MICHAEL KURLAND

CASTLE BOOKS

For Marcia Muller and Bill Pronzini,

with affection and gratitude, this book. . . may you find it useful.

This edition published in 2002 by
CASTLE BOOKS
A division of Book Sales, Inc.
114 Northfield Avenue
Edison, New Jersey 08837

Published by arrangement with
Hungry Minds, Inc
909 Third Avenue
New York, New York 10022

Library of Congress Cataloging-in-Publication Data
Kurland, Michael.
    How to try a murder : the armchair lawyer's handbook / Michael Kurland.

        p.   cm.
    Includes bibliographical references and index.
        1. Trials (Murder)—United States.   2. Criminal procedure—
United States.   3. Lawyers—United States—Handbooks, manuals, etc.

    I. Title.
KF9655.K87   1997   97-20974
345.7302'523—DC21   CIP

Printed in the United States of America

Book design by Nick Anderson

ISBN: 0-7858-1532-5

ACKNOWLEDGMENTS

I thank Linda Robertson for freely sharing her legal knowledge and for correcting as many of my mistakes and misconceptions as she could find.

I thank Olga Herrera Moya and Stephen Minch for their editorial assistance.

CONTENTS

MURDER ON TRIAL

> *"Do you mean to say that you . . . have let him live on after all those horrible deeds? . . . He deserves death."*
>
> *"Deserves it! I daresay he does. Many that live deserve death. And some that die deserve life. Can you give it to them? Then do not be too eager to deal out death in judgment. For even the very wise cannot see all ends."*
>
> — J.R.R. TOLKIEN
> *The Fellowship of the Ring*

For sheer human interest, the ability to catch public attention and cleave to it from start to finish, nothing else in real life equals a good murder trial. A prominent victim, or, even better, a prominent defendant; a bit of mystery surrounding the facts of the case; two prides of high-powered attorneys facing each other across the courtroom; a cluster of witnesses, each contributing a few tantalizing facts to a tale of human fallibility; a bevy of expert witnesses to explain the unexplainable; a man's or woman's life or freedom hanging in the balance—these are the makings of high drama. As Shakespeare taught us, good drama is an intimate mixture of both tragedy and farce.

This book will examine the roles of the various participants in a murder trial, from the defendant to the alternate jurors, and will show how the process functions and how an attempt is made to arrive at justice, if not truth, in this most serious of criminal procedures.

In *How to Solve a Murder* (Macmillan, 1995), I used a fictional murder to show how such a crime might be investigated by police and technical experts today, and how forensic evidence is collected and analyzed. Those components comprise the first half of the process that our society has evolved to deal with capital crimes. Much of the forensic technique, including not only the analysis of scientific evidence but also crime scene investigation procedures and the handling of physical evidence, has been developed within the past century and is still, almost daily, being improved and perfected.

This book will peer closely at courtroom procedure and strategy in a murder trial. The murder will be fictional and the trial hypothetical, but the process is typical of that in use throughout the United States today and is leavened with examples from real cases. The details of courtroom procedure vary from state to state, as each state jealously guards its right to run its judicial system as it pleases; but most of these procedures originate from a common source and are converging toward a common center as methods are standardized over time.

The criminal trial today is the fruit of a long and many-branched tree of legal thought and practice. It has roots in the Talmud, the book of Jewish law, which itself is rooted in ancient Babylon and the Code of Hammurabi. Its trunk is Roman law, and among its twined branches are Catholic Canon law, Anglo-Saxon practice, and Norman feudal law. These converged in English common law, the law of judges.

Instead of trying to craft written laws for every eventuality, English judges decided each case on the basis of precedent: What similar case had been tried before, and what had that judge decided? This allowed the law to evolve, as a judge could find that his case wasn't quite like the cases that had come before and needed a slightly different resolution. And, as each case was subject to the possibility of several levels of appeals, several judges would have the chance to see whether this case were truly the same as (or truly different from) the earlier cases, and whether the trial judge's rulings were lawful and just.

Appeals judges consider the proper application of the law rather than the guilt or innocence of the defendant. Unless compelling evidence is presented to the contrary, they assume that the jury that heard the evidence presented at the trial is normally the best judge of the facts. Even the existence of new evidence, unheard by the jury, is seldom cause to overturn a verdict. A substantive error in law or procedure, however, *will* overturn a guilty verdict and send the case back for retrial. I specify a "guilty" verdict because, once a defendant has been found innocent, he or she cannot be retried. To do so would violate the "double jeopardy" clause of the Fifth Amendment to the Constitution, which states in part: "nor shall any person be subject for the same offense to be twice put in jeopardy of life or limb."

THE IDEAL TRIAL

Through centuries of trial, and occasional error, an image of the ideal court has evolved toward which jurists strive. Its elements are an independent judge presiding over an adversary trial, in the presence of an unbiased jury, using established legal precedent to arrive at a just verdict. Let's briefly examine these points:

An Independent Judge

The judge should be independent of allegiance to anything but the law, favoring neither the prosecution nor the defense, and unswayed by public opinion or the desires of those who hold political office in his or her jurisdiction or any other.

An Adversary Trial

Truth has the best chance of emerging, jurists believe, when both sides of an issue are represented by intelligent advocates, trained in the law, who have equal chances of examining witnesses, analyzing evidence, objecting to improper testimony or actions of the opposing counsel, and presenting their clients' best face to the jury. The attorney's duty to the client is supposed to stop short of deliberate deception.

An Unbiased Jury

This is a jury of the defendant's "peers" who have no interest in the outcome of the trial except to see that justice is done. A defendant may choose to forego a jury, but having the option of a jury trial protects him or her from the "star chamber" of judges who are deciding at their ruler's behest.

Established Legal Precedent

A judge does not usually create his own law in relation to the admissibility of evidence, the questioning of witnesses, or any other aspect of the trial, but bases his decision on relevant statutory law or the principle of *stare decisis* (Latin for "stand by the decision"), which binds a judge to the decisions of the long line of past judges unless he has a very strong reason to dissent.

A Just Verdict

A just verdict is one based on the facts as presented in evidence. It is not necessarily the popular verdict.

In most murder trials the only person who knows the true story of the crime is the defendant, and then only if he or she is guilty. Circumstantial evidence is suspect, eyewitnesses are unreliable, forensic evidence is only as good as the laboratory that developed it. On the other hand, circumstantial evidence, if properly interpreted, can tell the story of the crime; eyewitnesses can be good observers; and a professionally run forensics laboratory can develop evidence that is trustworthy.

But these conditions may not be assumed. States' attorneys have been known to be overly zealous in pressing their case; defense attorneys have been known to be less dedicated, or less competent, than desired; and many people have spent years, even decades, in prison before a new circumstance showed that they were wrongly convicted. The recent introduction of DNA forensic analysis has already freed dozens of people who were shown to have been wrongly convicted—some on eyewitness testimony.

There is another side to this judicial coin: people who have committed murder and have been tried and found not guilty due to inadequate evidence, incompetent prosecution, a brilliant defense, or a jury not disposed to convict. That is, perhaps, a shame in the individual case, but it does society little harm in the long run, since no one would commit murder simply in the hope that his or her prosecution would be inept. Murder has the lowest recidivist rate of any major crime. It is much more likely that a mugger or a convenience-store robber will eventually kill someone than it is for a murderer found guilty of no other crime to kill again. It is my opinion that society would be more seriously harmed if the popular perception were that citizens were regularly convicted of crimes they did not commit.

There is no question that several score of people have been executed in this country during this century for crimes of which they were later shown to have been innocent. This seems not to have touched the consciences of those politicians and talk-show hosts who complain about the inordinate amount of time between sentencing and execution. While we dissect the murder trial, it may be well to keep in mind that the crime is so heinous because the loss is so great, and that no remedy is possible: one cannot restore the victim's life. Nor can the state restore the life of one mistakenly convicted and executed.

BENEFIT OF CLERGY

A curious holdover from medieval times that sneaked into the legal systems of many of the American colonies was the doctrine of "benefit of clergy." In Europe in the Middle Ages, with the domination of the spiritual over the secular in almost all spheres, a priest or monk accused of any crime could insist that he be tried in an ecclesiastical court. This was a useful protection in a day when the punishment for even minor crimes usually involved death or one of the unfriendlier forms of dismemberment. But if the accused was far from home with none to identify him, how could a man prove he was a cleric?

There was one way: The clergy knew how to read, and the laity, for the most part, did not. An accused person claiming the benefit of clergy could establish his spiritual bona fides by reading a passage from the Bible.

By the seventeenth century, the benefit had evolved into a general protection for the literate. If you could read the required passage from the Bible, you would be released with only a minor disfigurement—usually a letter branded on your thumb. And the case would not be turned over to the ecclesiastical court, but was merely dropped. The branded thumb assured that you could get away with committing a crime only once.

You didn't have to be very literate. The custom was for the Bible to be opened to Psalm 51 and for the miscreant to be asked to read the first few lines. Memorizing "Have mercy upon me, O God, according to thy loving-kindness: according unto the multitude of thy tender mercies blot out my transgressions" could literally turn out to be a lifesaver.

By the early eighteenth century in England and the various American colonies, particularly the southern ones, the benefit of clergy was extended to women, and, in 1732, the Virginia legislature not only included women in a benefit of clergy statute, but abolished the requirement that the claimer prove he or she could read. This effectively meant that anyone capable of memorizing a few lines of biblical verse (or, in Virginia, just remembering the magic words "benefit of clergy") could get away with murder at least once. To show they were serious when new criminal laws were passed, legislatures began writing in the statutes that penalties for certain offenses were "without benefit of clergy."

As late as 1784, one John Cullen was convicted of forgery, and the records show:

ON MOTION of Mr. Attorney-General [Cullen] was sent to the Bar for judgement, and it being demanded of him in the usual form what he could say for himself why judgement of death should not pass against him according to Law, he prayed the Benefit of Clergy, which was granted by the Court.

THEREUPON IT WAS ORDERED that the said John Cullen be branded in the brawn of the left Thumb with the letter T in the presence of the court, and that the sheriff execute the order immediately, which was done accordingly.

By the start of the nineteenth century the clergy had lost their benefit in all states, and literacy was no longer an acceptable defense against a charge of murder.

COURTROOM PERSONAE

During the course of a criminal trial many people with many different responsibilities are involved. Some serve in their official or professional capacity, and some by chance are caught up in the maw of justice. Many of these positions will be explored in greater detail later in this book, but it may be helpful to briefly outline their functions here.

The list includes:

The Defendant, who has been accused of and indicted for the crime, and whose legal guilt or innocence will be decided by the proceedings. If acquitted, the defendant will go free and cannot be tried for the same crime again. If found guilty, the defendant may be deprived of his or her liberty, or, in a capital case, life.

The Defense Attorney, or, if the defendant can afford it, the team of defense attorneys: the defendant's legal champions, who will use all of their skills to see that the defendant receives a fair trial and is acquitted of all charges. A defense attorney's reputation depends upon his or her ability to win cases.

The Prosecuting Attorney, who represents the state, and thus the people, and who believes that justice will be thwarted (and his or her own promising career damaged) if the defendant is allowed to escape unpunished for his or her heinous crime.

The Judge, who, as an impartial arbiter of the law, will decide what facts each side will be allowed to present into evidence and which witnesses each side will be allowed to call, and will also immediately rule on all questions regarding law or procedure. In the event of a guilty verdict, the judge must decide on the sentence, using sentencing guidelines established by the state. The guidelines of some states are more restrictive than others. In many states, capital murder sentences are decided by the jury in a separate proceeding after conviction.

The Court Clerk, an official of the court who takes care of all the court's business, including issuing subpoenas, marking and safeguarding evidence, handling paperwork, and keeping track of all documents and case records.

The Court Reporter, an employee of the court who, using a stenotype machine, takes down every word said as part of the testimony of the trial by the witnesses, the attorneys for both sides, and the judge. The court reporter also prepares official transcripts of each day's proceedings based on the stenotype record.

The Bailiff, the court's policeman, who is responsible for guarding the defendant if he or she is in custody, safeguarding the jury, and keeping the peace in the courtroom.

The Jury, comprised of twelve ordinary citizens, plus sometimes two or more alternate jurors in case of accident or dismissal, who decide the facts of the case as the judge decides the law. Only the jury can find a defendant guilty, although in certain circumstances a judge can override a jury and find a defendant innocent.

The Witnesses, those who sit in the witness box and give evidence and are sworn to tell the truth. They come in several different varieties: witnesses as to events concerning the crime in question, witnesses as to the character of the accused, and "expert" witnesses who can give opinions regarding medical, scientific, or other specialized evidence.

Let us look at how the cast of characters interacts in that real-life drama, the murder trial.

ONE

THE CRIME

> The majestic equality of the law forbids the rich as well as the poor to sleep under bridges, to beg in the streets, and to steal bread.

— ANATOLE FRANCE

It is mid-September, and the days are getting cooler in Metropolis, a moderate-sized city and capital of the Midwestern state of Arkham. The spate of summer crimes (burglaries, vandalism, hooliganism) is letting up, but for some crimes there is no season.

In the dark hours of a Tuesday night two of Metropolis's citizens have been brutally and cruelly murdered. That these citizens are socially prominent should not influence the prosecution of the crime, but it will. After a police investigation, a man is going to be accused of that murder, indicted, and tried. If he is found guilty, he could be sentenced to death. That the accused is both rich and socially important should not affect the course of justice, but it will.

The criminal law in Arkham is much like that in other states, and the court procedures in Metropolis resemble those in cities all over the United States. Let us follow this case and learn what we can as the accused and his advocates battle with representatives of the people of Arkham, with his life as prize.

DISCOVERY

Johansohn's Jewelers has been a fixture on Stately Street, here in Metropolis, for longer than any but the oldest residents can remember. It has discreetly served the

9

needs of Metropolis's husbands and lovers for many decades, even when, as happened on occasion, the customer was the husband of one lady and lover of another. It was eight o'clock on a dank, rainy Wednesday morning in September when Daniel Petrov, the store manager, entered through the front door and, after performing a few routine chores in preparation for the day's business, went to the back and found his boss, J.J. Johansohn, lying dead in his office.

Petrov stood and stared at his defunct employer for about a minute, unsure of what to do. J.J., lying sprawled near his desk clad only in his underwear, was unquestionably dead. His body was a mass of blood, which was also splattered about the office and slowly congealing in a pool about and under the body. It was not a lot of blood as such things go, but it was more than Petrov had ever seen before.

Petrov, usually the most unimaginative of men, was instantly certain that the killer was lurking somewhere about the store ready to add one more victim to his score. Summoning his courage, Petrov finally forced himself to retreat backward from the office, down the long aisle between the engagement and wedding ring counter and the silver plate and collectable china counter, to the telephone on the small desk at the break between the two. There he dialed 911, took a deep breath, and announced the fact of the murder clearly and precisely into the phone. Then he went into the bathroom and was sick.

Petrov's 911 call was put on the air, and a local patrol car was the first unit to arrive at the scene. Responding were Officers Abercrombie and Bull. Technically they then became the "first officers," and as such they had certain well-defined duties, which they performed. They were to secure the crime scene, verify that there was a corpse, conduct the initial interview of those present, keep the curious away, see that nothing was taken or changed, and await the detectives. It was while engaged in these routine tasks that Officer Abercrombie discovered that the office had a back room, that the back room had a couch, and that sprawled across it was another body—that of a woman clad only in a bra and panties. "Darn!" she said; that being the strongest expletive that Metropolis police officers ever use.

INVESTIGATION

Detectives Desilva and Brown from Central Squad, the group that worked out of Central Street Police Headquarters and investigated all major crimes in Metropolis, also answered the call. They looked over the crime scene and, wearing white latex gloves, carefully worked together to be sure that each could witness the other's actions if called upon to do so in court. Trying very carefully to obey the injunction to observe everything that might relate to the crime while disturbing nothing that might relate to the crime, they examined the bodies and the rooms containing them.

The body in the outer office was J.J. Johansohn. That was confirmed first by Petrov, and also by his resemblance to the man in the many photographs on the wall who was shaking hands with the great, the near great, and the notorious. It looked as though he had been shot, and more than once. Perhaps three times. The exact number, along with the caliber of the slugs and the path they took through the body, would await the medical examiner.

But who was the woman?

Detective Desilva crossed the office and entered the back room, walking as close to the wall as possible to preserve any footmarks or other evidence that might be on the floor further in the room. This room was more blood spattered than the office, possibly indicating that both victims had been shot in here and that J.J. had staggered—or had been dragged?—to the office to die. But at the time this was pure guesswork; it wasn't even officially established yet that the victims had been shot.

A handbag, presumably the dead woman's, was on an end table to one side of the couch. Desilva reached over carefully and picked it up by the strap. She reached inside with her latex-gloved hand to find the wallet. It was a combination wallet and checkbook, of some ultrasoft leather, heavy with credit cards and cash. She flipped it open and searched through the plastic card fan for a driver's license. For a long moment she stared at the laminated plastic card. Then she carefully backtracked out of the room and showed the license to her partner. "Golly," she said, that being her strongest epithet, "this is going to get interesting!"

"It certainly is," Brown agreed, staring mournfully down at the document. "As in the ancient Chinese curse: 'May you live in interesting times.'"

• • •

The case for the prosecution begins with the actions and observations of the detectives, and even the first officers, at the crime scene long before anyone is accused or even suspected of the crime. The state's attorney will be held liable by the defense for any mistakes made by the police anywhere along the line of the investigation, and its initial stages are the most vulnerable to errors of omission or commission. Besides providing ammunition for the defense, an overlooked or wrongly interpreted clue at the start of a case can point the detectives in the wrong direction and cost them momentum, even if it doesn't cause them to suspect the wrong person. The first 36 to 48 hours are the most important in a murder case, not only because the trail rapidly grows cold (although some murder cases have been solved decades after the crime), but also because the person the detectives focus on in those first two days is usually the person against whom they are going to develop a case. And if it is the wrong man, and unless he can afford a top attorney capable of spotting and pointing out these mistakes, he is just as likely to go to prison or be executed as the right man.

—In the O.J. Simpson trial, a detective wandering off to find a bloody glove by himself, a forensic technician neglecting to refrigerate a blood sample, and another detective keeping a vial of blood in his pocket gave the defense team some of the ammunition that they used to shoot up a smoke screen, which successfully obfuscated convincing forensic evidence and contributed to the ease with which the jury was able to acquit.

—In the 1954 trial of Doctor Sam Sheppard for the murder of his wife, it was not revealed that a policeman had flushed a toilet at the crime scene, sending down the drain a cigarette butt that had been floating in the bowl—even though neither the victim nor the accused smoked. Massive amounts of blood-splatter evidence also were either ignored or misinterpreted until years after the original conviction of Dr. Sheppard.

—When the Lindbergh baby was kidnapped in 1932, any traces of the perpetrators at the crime scene were obliterated by "[a] foaming and senseless cataract of gorgeously uniformed state troopers that descended on the Lindbergh home in motorcycles, roared up and down the road trampling every available clue into the March mud, systematically covering with impenetrable layers of stupidity every fingerprint, footprint, dust trace on the estate."[1]
These errors helped to create an unresolvable doubt as to whether the right man was convicted of the crime.

—During the first trial of Claus von Bülow for the attempted murder of his wife, Sunny, the prosecution made much of an insulin-encrusted hypodermic needle found by Sunny's son (Claus's stepson) in a black bag supposedly belonging to the accused. The theory was that Claus had injected her with it, causing an insulin-induced coma. The jury voted to convict. However, as was demonstrated at the retrial by

---

1. *Henry Morton Robinson:* Science Versus Crime.

Dr. Leo Dal Cortivo, a forensic toxicologist, the evidence had been misinterpreted; if that hypodermic had been used to inject Sunny, its passage through her skin would have wiped the outside clean. The most plausible way for it to have become coated with insulin was for someone to have dipped it in insulin and then left it to dry. Someone, perhaps, wanting to see Claus von Bülow convicted.

CORONERS

Although the office of coroner is just about defunct in the United States, in Great Britain, a coroner's inquest is held in any case of suspicious death. The coroner is responsible for ascertaining the cause of death, which may be accomplished with a post-mortem examination of the body and/or a formal inquest.

A HISTORY OF CORONERS

The office of coroner is the oldest existing position in English criminal law. The text *Jarvis on Coroners* (1829) refers to the Article of Eyre of 1194, at which time the office was already in existence. In 1276, the job of the coroner was described by statute in a document entitled *De Officia Coronatoris*:

> *A coroner should go to the place where any person is slain or suddenly dead or wounded, or where houses are broken, or where treasure is to be found, and should by his warrant to the bailiffs or constables summon a jury out of four or five neighboring towns to make inquiry upon view of the body; and the coroner and the jury should inquire into the manner of the killing.*

The office was imported to North America as the colonies were established. The coroner, usually with, but in some jurisdictions without, a coroner's jury, held an inquest over a person's death when there was any reason to assume that the death was other than natural. The inquest was to determine the cause of death and, in cases of murder or manslaughter, whether there was probable cause to suspect anyone of the crime. If probable cause was found, an indictment could be handed down and the suspect could be tried for the crime in a criminal court.

Coroner's inquests in the United States were commonly informal affairs. The coroner was usually a political appointee and was not required to be either a lawyer or a doctor. Often the town undertaker would get the job, as he was the one best equipped to deal with dead bodies. Those questioned at a coroner's inquest had no right to have an attorney present, although the coroner might allow it. The procedure for examining evidence and hearing witnesses in the coroner's court were those that the coroner chose and were designed to establish the basic facts in a case, not to definitely apportion guilt or innocence.

The office of coroner fell out of favor toward the end of the nineteenth century, as too many coroners were shown to be venal, corrupt, or incompetent. For a fee, a corrupt coroner might certify a suicide as an accidental death, allowing the relatives of the deceased to collect the life insurance. A coroner in Brooklyn, New York, who was paid by the inquest, had the body of a drowned man moved from place to place around the East River waterfront and held multiple inquests over the same corpse.

The office of coroner is disappearing around the United States, with coroners being replaced by medical examiners who are usually medical doctors trained in pathology. In some jurisdictions, such as Los Angeles County, the title of coroner is kept, but the position is filled by a trained forensic pathologist.

• • •

Desilva used her cell phone to make sure the forensic lab crew was on its way, and then called Captain Henderson, the commanding officer of Central Squad.

"We've got two bodies here, Cap," she told him. "One is J.J. Johansohn himself, the other is a Caucasian female in her late twenties. According to her driver's license, she is Lucille Lane. . . . That's right, Cap, the estranged wife of Broderick Lane."

Desilva listened stoically to her captain alternately whine and sputter at the other end of the connection.

"I understand," she said when he paused long enough to allow a response. "I'm sure Brown and I can handle it." More sputtering. "Yes, Cap," she told the phone. "Very careful. Ultra careful." She closed her cell phone and put it in her large black purse.

"We've got to go notify the husband," she told her partner. *"As soon as backup gets here."*

"Interesting times," Brown replied.

Broderick Lane, lately separated from his lovely wife, Lucille, was one of Metropolis's wealthiest and most important citizens: businessman, real estate magnate, owner of the local AFL franchise football team (the Metropolis Supermen). He was on every committee, council, and board of note in the state. A political enemy of Mayor Samson, he had supported the mayor's opponent in the last election.

Within half an hour backup arrived, in the form of two more Central Squad detectives and the forensics team. A minute later Detective Flanders, an investigator from the District Attorney's Major Crimes Bureau, joined them. Flanders was permanently attached to the Office of the District Attorney, and someone from his office worked with the police on every major crime as early in the investigation as possible. Flanders reminded the two detectives to be extra-careful in talking to Lane. District Attorney is also an elective office, and D.A. Adamson wanted to keep his political skirts clean.

Desilva and Brown drove off to locate Lane and inform him of his estranged wife's death. Although they now lived apart, Broderick and Lucille Lane were still married, and Broderick was her next of kin.

SUSPECT

It is perhaps a sad commentary that in our society the spouse of a murder victim is always the most logical suspect. But most homicides are committed by people known to the victim, and often the murderer is well known or related. When the detectives who notified O.J. Simpson that his wife, Nicole, had just been murdered swore in court that they did not think of Simpson as a suspect when they stood outside his estate, they were being less than ingenuous. They had no reason to think of him as an active suspect, which is what the defense would love to have established, because then they would have needed a warrant before they went over the wall and entered his property. But somewhere in the back of their minds there must have lurked the suspicion that the husband with a knife was a much more likely scenario than Colonel Mustard in the Drawing Room with a Candlestick.

• • •

Detectives Desilva and Brown found Lane in his office, where he professed to be shocked at the news of his wife's death. He claimed not to have seen his wife for three days. Where was he at the probable time of the murder? In bed asleep—alone. Did he own any handguns? Many, he was a collector. Would he take a nitrate test to see if he had fired a gun recently? He would, but it would be pointless; he had fired several weapons in his basement range at home yesterday. At this point Lane decided to stop answering questions and told the detectives that if they wanted to question him further, they would have to do so in the presence of his lawyer.

Meanwhile, back at the crime scene, the forensics crew—a senior forensics expert and a junior forensics expert—were slowly and carefully going over the area, picking up small bits of material to be identified later, carefully bagging them, and labeling them as to where and when they were found. They did the victims first so that the medical examiner could examine the bodies where they lay and then remove them to the morgue for post-mortem examination. At the same time, detectives were fanning out over the area for at least two blocks in every direction, trying to locate anyone who might have seen anything. These detectives would return that night, and over several more nights, to find possible witnesses who perhaps came out only at night and who might have been passing when the crime was committed. This commitment of personnel was more than what the average crime, or even the average murder, typically received.

• • •

Murders are the most heavily and carefully investigated of crimes, and the killing of the rich or famous commands even more of a police department's resources. This is not because celebrities or the wealthy intrinsically warrant deeper investigation, but, rather, because the level of defensive talent that the rich can hire, or the celebrity can inveigle, can play havoc with any mistakes made by the prosecution. The District Attorney's office, with its own investigators and the police department somewhat at its command, has vast resources. But those resources must be allocated over a great many criminal investigations. A talented defense attorney with an experienced staff and some capable private investigators—and the financial resources of a rich suspect to draw on—can easily equal the amount of investigation and preparation that the District Attorney can devote to even the most important case. There have, of course, been exceptions in cases where the crime was so heinous that someone had to be convicted for it, or where the crime received such public attention that the District Attorney had a political need to get a conviction. District Attorney is, after all, an elective office.

• • •

Two weeks later, Lane was arrested for the murder of his wife and J.J. Johansohn. He was taken before the nearest available magistrate and, as the state's attorney asserted that the indictment would be for first degree murder with special circumstances, a capital offense in Arkham, bail was denied and Lane was taken to jail.

THE ARREST WARRANT

The Criminal Complaint issued by the FBI against Timothy McVeigh in the matter of the bombing of the Federal Building in Oklahoma City:

1	UNITED STATES DISTRICT COURT
2	WESTERN DISTRICT OF OKLAHOMA
3	
4	UNITED STATES OF AMERICA, Criminal Complaint
5	Case Number: M-95-98-H
6	v
7	TIMOTHY JAMES McVEIGH
8	
9	
10	I, the undersigned complainant being duly sworn state the following is
11	true and correct to the best of my knowledge and belief. On or about April
12	19, 1995, in Oklahoma City, Oklahoma County, in the Western District of
13	Oklahoma defendant(s) did, maliciously damage and destroy by means of
14	fire or an explosive, any building, vehicle, and other personal or real prop-
15	erty in whole or in part owned, possessed, or used by the United States, any

1 department or agency thereof, in violation of Title 18, United States Code,

2 Section(s) 844(f).

3   I further state that I am a(n) Special Agent of the Federal Bureau of

4 Investigation and that this complaint is based on the following facts:

5   See attached Affidavit of Special Agent Henry C. Gibbons, Federal

6 Bureau of Investigation, which is incorporated and made a part hereof by

7 reference.

8   Continued on the attached sheet and made a part hereof: XX Yes No

9
                         /s/ Henry C. Gibbons
10   Signature of Complainant
                         HENRY C. GIBBONS
11   Special Agent
                         Federal Bureau of Investigation
12

13   Sworn to before me and subscribed in my presence, on this 21 day of

14 April, 1995, at Oklahoma City, Oklahoma.

15
                         RONALD L. HOWLAND
16   United States Magistrate Judge
                         /s/ Ronald L. Howland
17   Name and Title of Judicial Officer
                         Signature of Judicial Officer
18   STATE OF OKLAHOMA:
                         COUNTY OF OKLAHOMA

AFFIDAVIT

1   I, HENRY C. GIBBONS, being duly sworn, do hereby state that I am

2   an agent with the Federal Bureau of Investigation, having been so employed

3   for 26 years, and as such am vested with the authority to investigate viola-

4   tions of federal laws, including Title 18, United States Code, Section 844 (f).

5   Further, the Affiant states as follows:

6   1. The following information has been received by the Federal Bureau

7   of Investigation over the period from April 19 through April 21, 1995;

8   2. On April 19, 1995, a massive explosion detonated outside the Alfred

9   P. Murrah building in Oklahoma City, Oklahoma, at approximately 9:00 a.m.

10   3. Investigation by Federal agents at the scene of the explosion have

11   determined that the explosive was contained in a 1993 Ford owned by

12   Ryder Rental company.

13   a. A vehicle identification number (VIN) was found at the scene

14   of the explosion and determined to be from a part of the truck that con-

15   tained the explosive.

16   b. The VIN was traced to a truck owned by Ryder Rentals of

17   Miami, Florida.

18   c. Ryder Rentals informed the FBI that the truck was assigned to

19   a rental company known as Elliot's Body Shop in Junction City, Kansas.

20   4. The rental agent at Elliot's Body Shop in Junction City, Kansas was

21   interviewed by the FBI on April 19,1995. The individual who signed the

22   rental agreement provided the following information:

1   a. The person who signed the rental agreement identified himself

2   as BOB KLING, SSN: 962-42-9694, South Dakota's driver's license number

3   YF942A6, and provided a home address of 428 Malt Drive, Redfield, South

4   Dakota. The person listed the destination as 428 Maple Drive, Omaha,

5   Nebraska.

6   b. Subsequent investigation conducted by the FBI determine all

7   this information to be bogus.

8   5. On April 20, 1995, the rental agent was recontacted and assisted in

9   the creation of composite drawings. The rental agent has told the FBI that

10   the composite drawings are fair and accurate depictions of the individuals

11   who rented the truck.

12   6. On April 20, 1995, the FBI interviewed three witnesses who were

13   near the scene of the explosion at Alfred P. Murrah Federal Building prior to

14   the detonation of the explosives. The three witnesses were shown a copy of

15   the composite drawing of Unsub #1 and identified him as closely resembling

16   a person the witnesses had seen in front of the Alfred P. Murrah Building

17   where the explosion occurred on April 19, 1995. The witnesses advised the

18   FBI that they observed a person identified as Unsub #1 at approximately

19   8:40 a.m. on April 19, 1995, when they entered the building. They again ob-

20   served Unsub #1 at approximately 8:55 a.m., still in front of the 5th Road en-

21   trance of the building when they departed just minutes before the explosion.

22   7. The Alfred P. Murrah building is used by various agencies of the

23   United States, including Agriculture Department, Department of the Army,

24   the Defense Department, Federal Highway Administration, General

25   Accounting Office, General Services Administration, Social Security

26   Administration, Labor Department, Marine Corps, Small Business

1   Administration, Transportation Department, United States Secret Service,

2   Bureau of Alcohol, Tobacco and Firearms, and Veteran's Administration.

3   8. The composite drawings were shown to employees at various motels

4   and commercial establishments in the Junction City, Kansas, vicinity.

5   Employees of the Dreamland Motel in Junction City, Kansas, advised FBI

6   agents that an individual resembling Unsub #1 depicted in the composite

7   drawings had been a guest at the Motel from April 14 through April 18,

8   1995. This individual had registered at the Motel under the name of Tim

9   McVeigh, listed his automobile as bearing an Oklahoma license plate with

10   an illegible plate number, and provided a Michigan address, on North Van

11   Dyke Road in Decker, Michigan. The individual was seen driving a car

12   described as a Mercury from the 1970s.

13   9. A check of Michigan Department of motor Vehicle records shows a

14   license in the name of Timothy J. McVeigh, date of birth April 23, 1968,

15   with an address of 3616 North Van Dyke Road, Decker, Michigan. This

16   Michigan license was renewed by McVeigh on April 8, 1995. McVeigh had

17   a prior license issued in the state of Kansas on March 21, 1990, and sur-

18   rendered to Michigan in November 1993, with the following address: P.O.

19   Box 2153, Fort Riley, Kansas.

20   10. Further investigation shows that the property at 3616 North Van

21   Dyke Road, Decker, Michigan, is associated with James Douglas Nichols

22   and his brother Terry Lynn Nichols. The property is a working farm. Terry

23   Nichols formerly resided in Marion, Kansas, which is approximately one

24   hour from Junction City.

25   11. A relative of James Nichols reports to the FBI that Tim McVeigh is

26   a friend and associate of James Nichols, who has worked and resided at the

farm on North Van Dyke Road in Decker, Michigan. This relative further reports that she had heard that James Nichols had been involved in constructing bombs in approximately November 1994, and that he possessed large quantities of fuel oil and fertilizer.

12. On April 21, 1995, a former co-worker of Tim McVeigh's reported to the FBI that he had seen the composite drawing of Unsub #1 on the television and recognized the drawing to be a former co-worker, Tim McVeigh. He further advised that McVeigh was known to hold extreme rightwing views, was a military veteran, and was particularly agitated about the conduct of the federal government in Waco, Texas, in 1993. In fact, the co-worker further reports that McVeigh had been so agitated about the deaths of the Branch Davidians in Waco, Texas, on April 19, 1993, that he personally visited the site. After visiting the site, McVeigh expressed extreme anger at the federal government and advised that the Government should never had done what it did. He further advised that the last known address he had for McVeigh is 1711 Stockton Hill Road, #206, Kingman, Arizona.

13. On April 21, 1994, investigators learned that a Timothy McVeigh was arrested at 10:30 a.m. on April 19, 1995, in Perry, Oklahoma, for not having a license tag and for possession of a weapon approximately 1 1/2 hours after the detonation of the explosive device at the Alfred P. Murrah Federal Building in Oklahoma City, Oklahoma. Perry, Oklahoma, is approximately a 1 1/2 hour drive from Oklahoma City, Oklahoma. McVeigh, who has been held in custody since his arrest on April 19, 1995, listed his home address as 3616 North Van Dyke Road, Decker, Michigan. He listed James Nichols of Decker, Michigan, as a reference. McVeigh was stopped driving a yellow 1977 Mercury Marquis.

14. The detonation of the explosive in front of the Alfred P. Murrah Federal Building constitutes a violation of 18 U.S.C. Section 844(f), which makes it a crime to maliciously damage or destroy by means of an explosive any building or real property, in whole or in part owned, possessed or used by the United States, or any department or agency thereof.

Further, your affiant sayeth not.

/s/HENRY C. GIBBONS
Special Agent
Federal Bureau of Investigation

Subscribed and sworn to before me this 21 day of April 1995.

/s/ Ronald J. Howland
United States Magistrate Judge
Western District of Oklahoma

TWO

THE ARREST AND INDICTMENT

> *No person shall be held to answer for a Capital, or otherwise infamous crime, unless on a presentment or indictment of a Grand Jury . . .*
>
> —THE CONSTITUTION OF THE UNITED STATES, AMENDMENT V (1791)

A friend of mine, a New York criminal attorney whom I'll call Jack, who is an expert chess and bridge player, explained the criminal trial to me once years ago. It is a game, he said, played in deadly earnest between the two sides, with the judge as an impartial referee whose salary is being paid by the home team. For a few years Jack thought of the criminal trial as analogous to a game of *kriegspiel*, a German variant of chess in which neither player is allowed to see the board; but he came to realize that it more closely resembles poker: the cards you hold are not as important as the cards your opponent *thinks* you hold.

The attorneys for the state and for the defendant begin working out their strategies as soon as it appears that the case may go to trial—and often earlier. The prosecuting attorney's first decisions, after looking over the case and deciding that the accused is indeed guilty and that there is enough evidence to prove it to a jury, involve determining what testimony should be presented to the grand jury to get the indictment.

THE PLEA BARGAIN

Plea negotiations can happen any time from when the prospective defendant first talks to an attorney to the moment before the jury walks in with a verdict. The prosecution may offer to drop the charge from, say, first degree murder to manslaughter, and the defendant may then agree to plead guilty to the lesser charge. The prosecutor breathes a sigh of relief because she wasn't sure she could make the case, and at least the miscreant will be behind bars for a minimum of seven years. The defense attorney breathes a sigh of relief because he's not sure that the prosecution couldn't make the case, and he may have just saved his client from a lethal injection. The state is saved the considerable expense of a major felony trial.

As defense attorney Linda Robertson explains:

> There are exceptions, usually in serious cases where the district attorney is concerned with political fallout from seeming too lenient and feels he can win at trial, so he makes himself look tough by refusing to deal. But, in general, with courtroom space always in short supply and the possibility ever present of losing a case at trial and putting a suspected criminal back on the streets, judges and prosecutors are amenable to negotiation. Often deadlines are set by the prosecution after which no plea-bargaining will take place, but they're often honored in the breach, and cases have settled in chambers even as a jury panel waits in the courtroom. I've heard old-timers say that the sight of the jury can be a real incentive for some recalcitrant defendants to 'take the deal'.[1]

The plea bargain has been targeted by some politicians recently as one of the major flaws in our judicial system, along with indeterminate sentences and insufficient use of the death penalty, allowing miscreants to get away with serving lesser sentences than they deserve. Actually it is one of the strongest tools of the prosecution. By charging the defendant with a crime beyond that which they can actually prove, or for which they know that the evidence is weak or inadmissible—say it was illegally obtained—prosecutors can get guilty pleas in cases where they have less than a good chance of getting a conviction.

---

1. *Personal correspondence with author.*

GRAND JURY

The evidence against Broderick Lane was compelling, but was it good enough to get a conviction?

Lane had a history of abusing his wife. He had never broken any bones, but she had once needed nine stitches to close a gash in her cheek. There were medical records, but there was no police record. Being Broderick Lane, he had never been arrested for the assault. Lucille Lane had always refused to press charges, and the police had not pushed the matter. Even had there been an arrest record, it would probably not be admissible in court. But there was blood evidence and fingerprint evidence, and Lane did not have a useful alibi. Also, a witness saw a black Mercedes Benz leaving the alley behind the jewelry store at about 2:30 in the morning, within the time period the medical examiner places as the most probable for the murders to have been committed—and Lane owned a black Mercedes.

There was more, including witnesses to Lane's occasional bouts of uncontrollable jealousy and the family friend who claimed to have heard him say, "I'm going to kill that bitch someday." However, the reliability of these sources had not yet been determined.

District Attorney Adamson had to decide what bits of his case he would lay out to the grand jury. Just enough to get the indictment and no more. Even though grand jury testimony is taken in secret, Adamson knew he would have to hand over to the defense a transcription of the testimony of any witness he used in the trial; and there was no point in revealing any of his case to the defense unnecessarily. There was no chance that the grand jury would refuse to indict; the evidence was too clear for that. Besides that, as in most places, the grand jury was pretty much a tool of the prosecutor's office.

• • •

In federal courts, and in many states, an indictment must have been handed down by a grand jury before a person can be tried for a felony. Made up of 23 people (two regular juries minus one person, to avoid a tie vote) usually picked from regular jury rolls, a grand jury sits for one month to a year, depending on local law, and hears all the felony cases that are developed during that time. Its job is not to decide on the guilt or innocence of the accused, but merely to certify that there is enough evidence to conclude that a crime has been committed and that the accused was probably responsible and should be tried for the crime. The decision of a grand jury does not have to be unanimous; a simple majority is sufficient. This is an ancient procedure in English common law and descends from the assize, at which the knights assembled to hear criminal matters in the county. In federal courts, all felonies must be heard by a grand jury before an indictment—called in legal Latin a *billa vera*, or in English a "true bill"—can be issued. This protection is guaranteed by the Fifth Amendment to the Constitution, but the Supreme Court has ruled that states do not have to follow on this point. Many states do, but in some jurisdictions a grand jury is not necessary on all cases; instead a judge in a preliminary hearing can hand down an *information*, which is sufficient to bind the accused over for trial.

There are several differences between a preliminary hearing and a grand jury. A preliminary hearing is held without a jury, but it is public and is an adversarial proceeding. The defendant is present and is represented by his or her attorneys, who can cross-examine the witnesses and even, if they choose, present a defense. Grand jury proceedings are secret, and grand jurors can hear evidence that would probably be disallowed at a trial. In most states, if a witness who has testified at the grand jury hearing also testifies at the trial, the prosecution must give the defense a copy of that witness's grand jury testimony before the beginning of the cross-examination of that witness.

● ● ●

The grand jury listened carefully to the evidence presented by the district attorney's office and voted to hold Lane over for trial. The court clerk wrote out the indictment. Each state has different, although similar, rules for grand juries and forms for indictments. The one in Arkham read like this:

Court of General Sessions of the Peace in and for the County of Metropolis. The People of the State of Arkham against Broderick Wallingham Lane.

1. The People of the State of Arkham, by this indictment, accuse Broderick Wallingham Lane of the crime of murder in the first degree against Jeremiah Jesephat Johansohn, a human being and a citizen of the state of Arkham, a violation of Arkham Criminal Code Statute 102.4, in that he:

2. In the 17th day of September in the year of our Lord one thousand nine hundred and ninety-seven did go to the premises occupied by the Johansohn jewelry store, expecting to find Jeremiah Jesephat Johansohn present, and did with malice aforethought kill and murder Jeremiah Jesephat Johansohn with a gun or a knife, one or both weapons brought there for that purpose.

3. The People of the State of Arkham, by this indictment, further accuse Broderick Wallingham Lane of the crime of murder in the first degree against Lucille Kent Lane, a human being and a citizen of the state of Arkham, a violation of Arkham Criminal Code Statute 102.4, in that he:

4. In the 17th day of September in the year of our Lord one thousand nine hundred and ninety-seven did go to the premises occupied by the Johansohn jewelry store, expecting to find Lucille Kent Lane present, and did with malice aforethought kill and murder Lucille Kent Lane with a gun or a knife, one or both weapons brought there for that purpose.

5. This indictment includes all lesser crimes covered under the statute.

Prosecutors find the grand jury a useful tool for investigating a complex case, as the grand jury has subpoena power and can compel the testimony of anyone the prosecutor wants to question. The witness must also testify without the aid of an attorney. This has, on occasion, resulted in a witness repeatedly excusing himself to leave the room to consult with his lawyer waiting in the corridor.

Some prosecutors have misused the grand jury—going on "fishing expeditions"—to try to establish crimes of which they might not even have been aware at the start of the proceedings. Others have used "rubber stamp" grand juries to bring indictments against people they have no hope of convicting, either for personal publicity ("D.A. Tweetybird gets tough on crime, story at eleven.") or to harass the object of their disaffection. Occasionally, grand juries have taken control of the proceedings and thwarted overeager prosecutors, or forced investigations of things or people that the state's attorney would just as soon not have brought up. Such unilateral activity, however, is extremely rare.

Except in the federal court system, where the use of a grand jury is written into the Constitution, the grand jury is gradually withering away. Most states no longer use grand juries for minor offenses, and over a dozen have done away with them entirely. Many of them substitute a preliminary hearing in front of a magistrate.

INDICTMENT

A copy of the first part of the very long indictment of Theodore Kaczynski for the "Unabomber" bombings follows.

THE KACZYNSKI INDICTMENT

1 | Original Filed
June 18, 1996
2 | Clerk U.S. District Court
Eastern District of California
3 | By Deputy Clerk
CHARLES J. STEVENS
4 | United States Attorney
ROBERT J. CLEARY
5 | STEPHEN P. FRECCERO
BERNARD F. HUBLEY
6 | R. STEVEN LAPHAM
Special Attorneys to the United States Attorney General

7

8 | IN THE UNITED STATES DISTRICT COURT

9 | FOR THE EASTERN DISTRICT OF CALIFORNIA

10

11 | UNITED STATES OF AMERICA,   CR. No. S-CR-S-96-259 GEB
Plaintiff   Violations: 18 U.S.C.

12

13 | v

14 | THEODORE JOHN KACZYNSKI,
aka "FC"   Defendant

15

16 | Violations: 18 U.S.C. Section 844(d)—Transportation of an Explosive

17 | With Intent To Kill or Injure (4 Counts): 18 U.S.C. Section 1716—Mailing

18 | an Explosive

19 | Device With Intent to Kill or Injure (3 Counts) : 18 U.S.C. Section

20 | 924(c)(1)—Use of a Destructive Device In Relation to a Crime of Violence

21 | (3 Counts)

Indictment

I.

The Bomb That Killed Hugh Scrutton (Count 1)

Count One: [18 U.S.C. Sections 844(d) and 2(b)—Transportation of an Explosive With Intent to Kill or Injure]

The Grand Jury charges:

Theodore John Kaczynski

defendant herein, as follows:

1. In or about the fall of 1985, but not later than December 11, 1985, the defendant transported a bomb and bomb components from Montana to Sacramento, California. The defendant placed the bomb in the parking lot behind the rear entrance to Rentech, a computer store in Sacramento, California.

2. On or about December 11, 1985, Hugh Scrutton, the owner of Rentech, moved the bomb. This action caused the bomb to explode, killing Mr. Scrutton.

3. In or about the fall of 1985, but not later than December 11, 1985, in the State and Eastern District of California, and elsewhere, the defendant knowingly did transport and attempt to transport, and willfully did cause to be transported, in interstate commerce an explosive with the knowledge and intent that it would be used to kill, injure and intimidate an individual, and unlawfully to damage and destroy real and personal property, which did result in the death of Hugh Scrutton, in violation of Title 18, United States Code, Sections 844(d) and 2(b).

II.

The Bomb That Injured Dr. Charles Epstein (Counts 2–4)

Count Two: [18 U.S.C. Sections 844(d) and 2(b)— Transportation of an Explosive With Intent to Kill or Injure]

The Grand Jury further charges:

Theodore John Kaczynski

defendant herein, as follows:

4. From on or about June 16, 1993, to on or about June 18, 1993, the defendant transported a bomb and bomb components from Montana to Sacramento, California.

5. On or about June 18, 1993, the defendant mailed the bomb from Sacramento, California to Dr. Charles Epstein in Tiburon, California. The bomb was contained in a wooden box, placed in a padded mailing envelope. The package containing the bomb was delivered to Dr. Epstein's home.

6. On or about June 22, 1993, while in his home, Dr. Epstein opened the package referred to in paragraph 5, causing it to explode and injure him.

7. From on or about June 16, 1993, to on or about June 22, 1993, in the State and Eastern District of California, and elsewhere, the defendant knowingly did transport and attempt to transport, and willfully did cause to be transported, in interstate commerce an explosive with the knowledge and intent that it would be used to kill, injure and intimidate an individual, and unlawfully to damage and destroy real personal property, which did result in personal injury to Dr. Charles Epstein, in violation of Title 18, United States Code, Sections 844(d) and 2(b).

1 **Count Three:** [18 U.S.C. Section 1716—Mailing an Explosive Device With

2 Intent to Kill or Injure]

3 The Grand Jury further charges:

4 Theodore John Kaczynski

5 defendant herein, as follows:

6

7   8. Paragraphs 4–6 are repeated and realleged as though set forth in full.

8   9. On or about June 18, 1993, in the State and Eastern District of

9 California, and elsewhere, the defendant knowingly did deposit for mailing

10 and delivery and knowingly did cause to be delivered by mail, according to

11 the direction thereon, nonmailable matter, to wit: a device and composition

12 which could ignite and explode, with the intent to kill and injure another,

13 in violation of Title 18, United States Code, Section 1716.

14

15 **Count Four:** [18 U.S.C. Section 924 (c)(1)—Use of a Destructive Device In

16 Relation to a Crime of Violence]

17 The Grand Jury further charges:

18 Theodore John Kaczynski

19 defendant herein, as follows:

20

21   10. Paragraphs 4 through 6 are repeated and realleged as though set

22 forth in full.

23   11. From on or about June 16, 1993, to on or about June 22, 1993, in

24 the State and Eastern district of California, and elsewhere, during and in

25 relation to a crime of violence for which he may be prosecuted in a court of

26 the United States, to wit: transportation of an explosive with intent to kill

1 and injure and mailing an explosive device with intent to kill and injure, as

2 charged in Counts Two and Three, the defendant knowingly did use and

3 carry a firearm, that is, a destructive device, in violation of Title 18, United

4 States Code, Section 924(c)(1).

TO DILIGENTLY ENQUIRE. . .

The most ancient archive of the Court of General Sessions in the Colony of New York records, on its first page, the empaneling of a grand jury:

PROVENCE OF NEW YORK. Att the General Quarter Sessions of our Lord the King held att the Citty Hall in the Citty of New-York for Our Sayd Lord the King, and the body of the sayd Citty and County of New-York, that is to say on Tuesday the 8th day of February, in the Six and Thirtieth year of the Reigne of our Sovereigne Lord Charles the Second of England, Scottland, France and Ireland, King, Defender of the faith, & before Cornelis Steenyck, Esqr, May^r of the sayd Citty, and James Graham, Recorder, Nicholas Bayard, John Inians, Wm Pinho...Guyl. Ver Plank, Jno Robinson and William Cox, Esq^{rs}, Aldermen and Justices of the Peace of the sayd Citty and County, Commisionated by Authority und^r his Royal Highness James Duke of York and Albany Lord Propriet^r of the Province afores^d....

The Grand Jury...was called and sworne According to An Oath Agreed On by the Court, and was as followeth, viz^{tt}.:

"You shall diligently Inquire and true Presentm^t make of all Such things and matt^{rs} as shall be giuen you in Charge Or shall Come to your knowledge this Present Servise. The Kings, His Royal Highness Lord Propriet^r and this City Councell Yo^r fallows and you^r owne you shall well and Truely keep secreet. You shall present nothing for Malace or Euill will that you Bare to Any Person, Neither shall you Leaue anything unpresented for Loue, Favour, Affecttion Reward Or Any hopes thereof, but in all things that shall Concerne this Present Servise you Shall Present the truth the whole truth and nothing but the truth, According to yor best skill and knowledge--Soe help you God.

M^r. Francis Rumbout was apoynted foreman.

This first case was against one Henry Thomassen, who was charged with burglary. The grand jury brought a true bill against him, and was then informed by the "Sherriff" that Mr. Thomassen had "Broak Prison." The "Sherriff" was ordered to "Persue him." He caught him, and the felon was tried at the next session. The record for that session, unfortunately, is missing.

DEFENSE ATTORNEY

Before his arrest, when it became clear that the police were interested in him as a suspect, Broderick Lane had gone to his attorney, Mal Geldfresser, of the respected firm of Frottage, Pickelhaub & Geldfresser, and said, "Mal, I need help. I think I'm going to be accused of murdering my wife."

"Did you do it?" Mal asked. Then he quickly threw up his hands in horror. "Don't answer that! I shouldn't have asked, and I don't want to know the answer."

"You don't want to know whether I killed my wife or not?" Lane asked incredulously.

"It doesn't concern me. I can't represent you in this anyway, so I have no reason to know. Whoever does represent you might not want to know either."

"You've been my attorney for twenty years, and now that I'm really in trouble . . . "

"You need a trial attorney who is experienced in handling criminal cases, not a corporate attorney who's expert in drawing up contracts. We don't have anyone like that in our firm. Let me make some phone calls."

"Who's the best?" Lane asked. "I want the best."

Mal picked up the phone. "I'll call Artemus Porter."

• • •

Being a criminal defense attorney is a very specialized calling. Most lawyers seldom speak in open court, and many go through their entire career without ever entering a criminal courtroom. The top defense attorneys are often loners, both because that fits in with their personality and because major law firms consider it somehow disreputable to have a criminal lawyer among the partners. This prejudice has been somewhat reduced in the current age of corporate malfeasance and white-collar crime. A top law firm today might include a criminal litigation expert to represent a client who has bilked a few thousand widows and orphans of a few million dollars, but there is probably no one in the firm capable of or interested in representing the hungry man accused of stealing a loaf of bread.

• • •

Broderick Lane had never met anyone like Artemus Porter. The famed trial attorney was short and stocky, with an unruly shock of graying hair, a prominent nose and a wide mustache. He wore extra-wide suspenders, which he had in a variety of colors. Porter had a hat collection, with thirty or forty hats hanging on pegs around his office. Before leaving, he would pick one and jam it on his head. Grisly souvenirs of past cases filled cabinets around the office, along with exotic or merely strange gifts given him by past clients. There was a moose head sitting on a table so it stared up at the ceiling, an articulated skeleton, a fire ax, a skull with a neat bullet hole through the front and out the back (having entered the frontal bone and exited through the occipital bone, as Porter explained).

"Tell me something about yourself," Porter said. "But not about the case, we'll save that."

"Don't you even want to know if I'm guilty?" Lane asked, a little annoyed that nobody seemed to care about what was to him the most important fact in the proceedings.

Porter sat Lane down and explained to him some things that he never had to think about before.

The Ethics of Defense

There is an interesting moral and/or ethical problem faced by all defense attorneys, one from which the prosecution is exempt. It is their job to defend their clients to the best of their abilities, doing all in their power within the strictures of the Canon of Ethics of the Bar Association to see that their client is acquitted. The theory is that an open adversarial proceeding, with the attorneys of both sides free to flail away at each other and their theories of the crime, their physical evidence and their witnesses under the watchful eye of the judge, is the best way of influencing a panel of twelve pressed citizens to arrive at a just and reasonable verdict. The attorneys are not to knowingly allow a sworn witness to lie, although they can stretch the truth themselves in their summation—they, after all, have not been sworn.

But let us suppose that, while preparing his client's case, a defense attorney hears something he doesn't want to hear.

> Who killed Cock Robin?
> "I," said the Sparrow.
> "With my bow and arrow,
> "I killed Cock Robin."

If that admission were made by Sparrow to his defense attorney, the attorney would have a problem. As an officer of the court, he should reveal Sparrow's admission to the District Attorney, or at least to the court (which would mean the judge). But it is agreed that the attorney-client relationship would forbid him to do any such thing without his client's express permission. If the Sparrow wants a defense, a defense he must have, even though the attorney now knows the entire defense will be an exercise in mendacity.

However, even the attorney-client privilege would not suffice to allow the attorney to put his client on the stand knowing he was going to lie under oath. (Also, it should be noted that the lawyer-client privilege ceases to exist "if the lawyer reasonably believes that disclosure of any confidential communication relating to representation of a client is necessary to prevent the client from committing a criminal act that the lawyer believes is likely to result in death or substantial bodily harm.")[2]

Since lawyers do on occasion defend guilty clients—though as many lawyers have pointed out no defendant is guilty until a jury says so—there are several ways around this dilemma. A lawyer is not required to believe his client. If the attorney can convince himself that his client was lying to protect someone else, or out of a neurotic need to confess, or for whatever reason, then he can feel completely justified in ignoring his client's confession. Another option, one used by many trial lawyers, is to never allow the client to tell his story. They develop instead a series of hypotheses about the crime that would explain away the physical evidence and the eyewitness testimony without ever inquiring as to what the truth—or the client's version of the truth—might be. If the defense attorney can come up with an alternate version

---

2. *California Evidence Code: 956.5.*

of events that would explain all the evidence, he doesn't have to prove it, but can merely suggest it and convince one member of the jury that it is as probable as the prosecution's version. It is not the defense attorney's job to prove anything, but merely to debunk the prosecutor's story. As Arthur Train put it some ninety years ago:

> . . . the prisoner is entitled to every reasonable doubt, even from his own lawyer. It is the lawyer's business to create such a doubt if he can, and we must not be too censorious if, in his eagerness to raise this in the minds of the jury, he sometimes oversteps the bounds of propriety, appeals to popular prejudices and emotions, makes illogical deductions from the evidence, and impugns the motives of the prosecution. (*Courts and Criminals*)

Sometimes the "bounds of propriety" can be made to work for the defense. In the famous case of Lizzie Borden (Fall River, Massachusetts, August 4, 1892), her father and stepmother were found hacked to death in their house. The only people present were Lizzie, who claimed to be out in the barn behind the house looking for lead for sinkers, although there was no evidence that she intended to go fishing; and Bridget, the maid, who was resting in her room between chores. Anyone else who tried to enter the house would surely have been seen by people loitering on their porches on this hot midsummer day. Lizzie was shown to have had constant fights with her stepmother and a recent dispute with her father. There was, if not a river, at least a stream of circumstantial evidence against her. Besides, it did not seem physically possible for anyone else to have committed the crime. Her attorney's defense at the trial was that a well-brought-up Victorian lady (Lizzie was 32 at the time) could not possibly do such a thing. Lizzie was acquitted.

The children of Fall River perhaps had a better idea of what a Victorian lady was capable of doing. Within weeks after the trial, they were chanting the now immortal:

> Lizzie Borden took an axe
> And gave her mother forty whacks,
> And when she saw what she had done
> She gave her father forty-one!

Let's look at another scenario. Let us assume that the police searched the home of a murder suspect and found the murder weapon, with the suspect's fingerprints on it, hidden under his mattress. Let us further assume that they confront the suspect with this material and he breaks down and gives a lengthy and detailed confession, citing facts about the killing that only the murderer could have known.

Now, as the date for the trial approaches, the defense attorney goes to the judge with a motion to exclude the weapon and the confession from the trial evidence. Let us say that the search warrant was faulty, and the confession was obtained when the suspect's lawyer was absent, although he had requested that he not be questioned without his lawyer present. There is a good chance that the judge will disallow both the weapon and the confession.

In the opposite situation, if someone else's fingerprints were found on the weapon, or someone else confessed, the prosecutor could then merely dismiss the case and apologize to the defendant for the inconvenience. There is no ethical or moral stretch for him to realize he was mistaken. As prosecutors should occasionally remind themselves, the people and justice are best served when the truth is discovered, whether that results in the conviction or the release of a defendant.

But the defense attorney cannot drop the case in a situation where he, the prosecutor, the judge, and indeed everyone in the courtroom but the jury is certain that the defendant is guilty. He must proceed as though the disallowed weapon does not exist and the confession were never uttered, continuing in the knowledge that if he loses the case he has failed at his job, and if he wins he has loosed a murderer on the community.

CUMMINGS THE JUST

In Bridgeport, Connecticut, on February 4, 1924, Father Hubert Dahme, pastor of St. Joseph's Episcopal Church, was accosted on the street and shot dead. The city was outraged, and the police were under pressure to arrest someone. They apprehended a 23-year-old drifter from Pennsylvania named Harold Israel, who had a gun of the same caliber as the bullet that had killed Father Dahme. They questioned Israel for some time in the back room of the police station until he confessed.

The gun was tested by a ballistics expert, who certified that it was the murder weapon. The police located some witnesses who had seen Israel do the killing.

This was the case that was handed to state's attorney Homer S. Cummings to prosecute, and no prosecutor has ever been handed a neater bundle. The public wanted a quick conviction, and the evidence was in his hand to secure one. Cummings, a very popular prosecutor, was being seriously thought of as the next Democratic candidate for governor, and successfully prosecuting the murderer of the well-liked priest would not hurt his chances.

Israel tried to retract his confession, claiming that the police had not let him sleep and that he had been exhausted, hungry, and bewildered by the constant police pressure when he made it. But every defendant disowns every confession with some similar excuse. The defense attorney saw little hope for his client and planned to plead not guilty by reason of insanity.

But something about the case smelled. Cummings detected the odor of lying witnesses and became convinced that the confession had truly been coerced. But what of the ballistics evidence? Cummings sent the gun and bullet out to six different ballistics experts without telling any one of them about the others. Every one of them came to the independent conclusion that the bullet that killed Father Dahme had not been fired from Israel's gun. There was also, they discovered, a mechanical flaw in the weapon.

In his opening statement at the trial, Cummings outlined the facts of the case as he knew them. He pointed out that because of lighting conditions, the witnesses could not have seen what they claimed to have seen; he demolished the police's ballistic expert with six experts of his own; and then he loaded Harold Israel's pistol, pointed it at the floor, and pulled the trigger. The gun refused to fire. It had a defective firing pin and would not fire at the angle at which the murder weapon must have been held when Father Dahme was shot.

The judge directed that Israel be released, and Cummings personally took him to the train station. The townspeople, who wanted someone punished for Father Dahme's murder, somehow felt cheated over their prosecutor failing to prosecute, and Cummings was never elected Governor. Unpopular though his actions might have been at the time, they are truly representative of the American ideal of justice. Cummings became Attorney General of the United States under President Franklin D. Roosevelt.

The story of Homer Cummings' search for truth while a prosecuting attorney inspired the 1947 film *Boomerang*, starring Dana Andrews and directed by Elia Kazan. No one was ever tried for the murder of Father Hubert Dahme.

THREE

TRIAL PREPARATION

> The charge is prepar'd; the lawyers are met; The Judges all rang'd
> (a terrible show!).
>
> ———— JOHN GAY
> *The Beggar's Opera*

THE PROSECUTION

The prosecution of State of Arkham v Lane *promised to be a political land mine. Regardless of the ultimate disposition of the case, whether millionaire real estate magnate Broderick Lane were found innocent or guilty, the prosecutors were going to have to appear absolutely even-handed and fair. How to appear even-handed when you're trying to put someone in prison for the rest of his life—or take his life—would require some delicate juggling.*

District Attorney Adamson turned the case over to his most experienced and capable trial attorney, Assistant D.A. Carter Weiss, and then isolated himself from it, at least in public. When questioned about it Adamson would insist that it was being handled in a normal, routine fashion by his staff, and that he had absolute confidence in any decisions that his trusted associate Carter Weiss might make. Weiss, known as "The Wizard" around the office for his ability to construct airtight cases and win convictions, received pep talks from Adamson at least twice a day, alternated with warnings as to what would happen to him if he screwed up.

Weiss had many decisions to make as he prepared his case. One of the first was just what to charge Broderick with. The State's contention was that it was first degree

murder, that Lane went to the shop with a strong reason to kill his wife and her para-
mour, with the intention of killing them, and was prepared to kill them, and that, fol-
lowing his preconceived plan, he then committed the act. But it wasn't that simple;
there were other considerations.

Murder Defined

The crime of murder, as with most crimes, is left to the individual states
to define and punish, with the exception that the Federal Government
takes enforcement responsibility for killings that take place on federal
lands or military bases. Indian reservations are also under federal jurisdiction, but much of the law on reservations is administered by tribal
councils and enforced by tribal police forces. The Federal Government
also reserves for itself such potentially capital offenses as treason and
the rather strangely conceived crime of depriving individuals of their
civil rights by killing them. Under recently enacted federal statutes, an
act of terrorism that results in a death is now a capital crime. Murders
committed by what President Clinton described as "drug kingpins and
police killers" are also capital crimes.

The states all define murder similarly, and most, in an effort to
adjust the penalty to fit the crime, have broken the definition of the
killing of one human being by another into six categories: murder in
the first degree, murder in the second degree, manslaughter in the first
degree, manslaughter in the second degree, justifiable homicide, and
accidental death. In some states the names are different, and specific
crimes such as vehicular homicide may be put into one class or another, but such differences are minimal.

Murder in the first degree is the willful, deliberate and premeditated killing of one person by another. The murderer intends to kill the
victim, plans to kills the victim, and acts with "malice aforethought,"
which is the existence of a state of mind that causes one to intentionally commit the act. Premeditation means that the plan existed before
the act, but the premeditation does not have to be of long duration,
just long enough to give the killer time to consider the gravity of his or
her act; going into another room to get the weapon is sufficient. A
killing for hire is first degree murder for both the actual killer and the
one who did the hiring.

"Felony murder," a killing caused by or during the commission of a
felony specified by statute, usually including armed robbery, arson,

burglary, kidnapping, and rape, is treated as first degree murder. If Bartlesby sticks up a pilchard shop and the owner reaches for his pepperpot pistol, and Bartlesby shoots and kills him, this is first degree murder even though Bartlesby did not intend to harm anyone when he entered the shop. If Bartlesby trips on his way to the counter and his gun discharges accidentally and kills the owner, this also is felony murder.

If Bartlesby and Ormand rob the pilchard shop together, and the owner pulls out his pepperpot pistol and Ormand kills the owner, both Bartlesby and Ormand, and even Sigismund, who was outside driving the getaway car and didn't even know Ormand had a gun, can be tried for felony murder. Curiously, if Bartlesby and Ormand rob the pilchard shop together, and Ormand threatens the owner with his gun, and the owner pulls out his pepperpot pistol and kills Ormand, Bartlesby can be tried for murder, since the owner acted in self-defense and it was Bartlesby's felonious actions that resulted in the death of Ormand. To take these convolutions one step further: if Ormand threatens the owner, who grabs a customer to use as a shield, and Ormand kills the customer, Ormand, Bartlesby, and the owner can all be tried for murder; but if the owner merely ducks behind a customer without touching him, and the customer is killed, the owner is not guilty of anything.

Although "malice aforethought" is a necessary ingredient of first-degree murder, the presence of malice would not turn another sort of killing, say self-defense, into first-degree murder:

> Whenever the circumstances of the killing would not amount to murder, the proof even of express malice will not make it so. One may harbor the most intense hatred toward another; he may court an opportunity to take his life; may rejoice while he is imbruing his hands in his heart's blood; and yet, if, to save his own life, the facts showed that he was fully justified in slaying his adversary, his malice shall not be taken into account.
>
> —*Golden v Georgia*, 25 GA. 527, 532 (1858).

Murder in the second degree is a killing in which malice aforethought is present, but premeditation is absent. Behaving "with reckless indifference to human life" in a manner that results in a death is second-degree murder. A homicide committed during the course of a felony that is not among those specified by statute to be first-degree felony murder can be second-degree murder. Parents who abuse children with fatal results can be prosecuted for second-degree murder. Sometime long ago a dentist in California who negligently killed a couple of his patients with a general anesthetic was found guilty of second-degree murder.

Manslaughter in the first degree, also known as voluntary manslaughter, is the intentional killing of another with the element of malice missing. Killing while in the grip of extreme passion, hate, rage, or jealousy, directed at the victim but not planned, can be voluntary manslaughter if the victim has done something to provoke the hate, rage, or jealousy. If Rosencrantz taunts Guildenstern about his funny name until Guildenstern, in a rage, stabs and kills Rosencrantz, that can be manslaughter in the first degree. But note that if Guildenstern goes out to his dog cart to get his dagger and then comes back and slays Rosencrantz, he has now premeditated the act and it has become first-degree murder. If Guildenstern slays Rosencrantz in the honest belief that he is acting in self-defense, but that belief is shown to be unreasonable, Guildenstern has committed manslaughter in the first degree.

Manslaughter in the second degree, or involuntary manslaughter, occurs when someone has caused the death of another as the result of grossly negligent or reckless acts that carry a high risk of seriously injuring or killing another. This is also known as "criminally negligent homicide." Unreasonable or grossly negligent conduct, such as waving a loaded gun around, that results in a death is also involuntary manslaughter. Throwing bricks off an overpass onto oncoming traffic would, if it resulted in a death, also be an example.

WHAT IS THIS THING CALLED MURDER?

The word *murder* comes from the Middle English *murther*, by way of Old French, with Latin and Greek root words meaning "death" or "to die," and possibly with a hint of the Old English *morth*, meaning "secret." In a time when life tended to be brief and killing was common, a murder was a killing done in secret, "whereof it cannot be known by whom it was done" (Britton, c.1290), thus making it impossible for the relatives of the victim to attain either recompense or revenge.

For the first few centuries after the Norman Conquest, feudal obligations defined which killings were murders and how such killings should be avenged. A man's primary obligation was to his lord, and if he killed in defense of his lord, or of a close female relative, this was not considered murder and no action would be taken against the man. If a man killed a thief in the act of getting away, he was exempt from retribution. For other killings, depending on the victim and the circumstance, a sentence might be pronounced upon the perpetrator ranging from death to compensation for the victim's relatives in money or goods. A killing from ambush or by poison was a capital crime. Other killings were punished by payment of a specified amount, called a *bot*, of which one part (the *wite*) went to the victim's relatives and the other (the *wer*) to the king. The question "What is the value of a man's life?" was very carefully worked out in criminal law then, as it is in civil law today.

As English common law evolved, the legal meaning of *murder* narrowed, becoming the unlawful killing of another human being "with malice aforethought." This meant that for a homicide to be murder, the killer had to have planned the killing, however briefly, and have felt some animosity toward the victim. The American colonies naturally adopted English common law, and they maintained it after the Revolution. Civil law was not so consistent. In Louisiana, which derived its laws from the *Code Napoleon*, and in California and New Mexico, whose Mexican heritage includes a good bit of Spanish law, the civil codes differ from the rest of the country, especially in regard to real property (community property, for example, is a Spanish notion). But the criminal law in all the states and the federal government is still firmly rooted in English common law.

The Charge

Assistant District Attorney Weiss had an interesting problem in determining just what the charge against Broderick Lane should be. Two counts of first degree murder, yes; but the option of including lesser counts of second degree murder must be considered. And, in case the jury found Lane guilty of "murder one," as Weiss thought probable, should the charge allege special circumstances, which would make Mr. Lane eligible for the death sentence under the laws of Arkham?

Under Arkham's criminal codes, any or none of the above could be done at the discretion of the prosecutor. That's why the indictment included paragraph 5: "This indictment includes all lesser crimes covered under the statute." But Weiss had to consider the effect the specific charges in the indictment would have as he presented his case to the jury.

•   •   •

Including a charge of second degree murder with a charge of first degree murder, when the charges are directed at the same defendant for killing the same victim, is not an exercise in redundancy; it is a result of the formalistic precision the law demands in its working. Our fictitious Arkham is one of the states in which a defendant can be convicted only of the specific crime with which he or she is charged. If a jury is convinced that the defendant committed the murder, but that one of the necessary elements to make it first degree—say, the malice aforethought—is missing, or insufficiently proven, then they cannot find that person guilty of murder in the first degree. If a second-degree charge is included in the indictment, the jury can find the defendant guilty of that, but if it isn't, they must find the person innocent. The prosecutor also cannot retry the defendant for murder in the second degree, as that would put him or her in jeopardy twice for the same crime. In some states, however, such as California, this is not so, and even when the charging document charges first-degree murder, the jury is permitted to find the defendant guilty of second-degree murder or even manslaughter, if that is the way they read the evidence.

A peculiarity of this allowance in California is that if the jury finds the defendant guilty of "murder" without further specifying, the finding must be assumed to be second-degree murder, not first. California courts avoid the possibility of this by supplying the jury with printed forms that state the degree. But what happens when the jury fails to properly fill out the form?

—On September 25, 1987, Billy Paul Birdwell II was found guilty of the murder of Douglas Leroy Jensen. Special circumstances were alleged and the jury agreed: the murder happened during the commission of a robbery, and "a deadly and dangerous weapon, a knife" was used. Birdwell was sentenced to state prison for life without the possibility of parole, a first-degree murder with special circumstances sentence.

The jury's decision covers the first three paragraphs of that jury's verdict form. But the foreperson, or whoever was filling out the form, forgot to check either box of Paragraph 4:

> 4. We further find that the murder is of the___FIRST___SECOND degree.

In November 1996, the California Court of Appeal found that the wording of the California statute does not allow for the "true intent" of the jury if a mistake is made, ruling that "[T]he net effect . . . is that the jury found petitioner guilty of only second degree murder. We are reasonably certain that the jury will be surprised to learn of its 'new' verdict. We are also reasonably certain that the sentencing court will be surprised to learn that it imposed a first degree murder sentence for a second degree murder."

It would seem obvious that, in states where the degree must be specified on the indictment, the lesser crime should always be included with the greater as a fall-back position. But, as one might expect when dealing with questions of human behavior, it isn't that simple. Second-degree murder is too easy a fall-back position for juries who find themselves deadlocked. Say ten jurors think that defendant Burke is guilty of premeditated murder—that he did knock several old men over the head to sell their bodies to medical science. Say that two jurors aren't convinced. They think that his story of just finding the bodies lying predeceased on the street might be true. If lower charges are included, the jury might compromise just to break the deadlock and go home to dinner. But the prosecutor, who knows for certain that Burke is guilty because of the confession of Burke's partner Hare, which unfortunately is inadmissible in court, doesn't want to give the jury this option. He'd rather have them spend an extra day in the jury room fighting it out until they come up with a conviction. If he only could be sure . . .

The assertion of "special circumstances" is necessary in order to ask for the death penalty in a first-degree murder. This is due to a Supreme Court decision that will be discussed in Chapter Eight.

The Plea

Artemus Porter also has decisions to make. His client claims he is innocent and has no intention of pleading guilty. "If I wanted to plead guilty," Lane told Porter, "I would have gotten a cheaper lawyer."

Hypothetically, Porter does not have to present any defense and does not have to put the defendant on the stand. All he has to do is to so discredit the prosecution's witnesses as to introduce into the minds of the jurors a reasonable doubt. This has worked, but it is dangerous; jurors need to have some theory of the crime, and if they are not to believe what is offered by the prosecution, then the defense must offer an alternative. Porter pondered.

•   •   •

The job of a jury is to find the defendant innocent or find him guilty "beyond a reasonable doubt." But a jury is an assemblage of human beings, and when presented with problems, human beings want answers. Consequently, most defense attorneys feel that they have to present the jury with a reasonable alternative to the prosecution's theory of the case.

Sometimes even the best attorney will plead his client guilty. In the 1924 trial of Nathan Leopold and Richard Loeb, teenage boys from rich Chicago families, for the "thrill killing" of 14-year-old Bobby Franks, the boys' families hired Clarence Darrow, the most famous and one of the most able trial lawyers of the first half of the century, to defend them. Darrow, 67 years old, tired, and in pain from a variety of ailments, didn't want to take the case. But he was an adamant foe of the death penalty, and with anyone less than Darrow as their counsel, the boys would probably hang. Even Darrow, who hadn't lost a man to the gallows in over 100 capital cases, would not have an easy time of it.

In looking over the evidence, which included confessions from both boys (although each said the other did the actual killing—a moot point, as each was equally culpable under the law) and a wide swath of corroborating circumstantial evidence, Darrow realized that it was unlikely that he could convince a jury of his clients' innocence. And once they were convicted of a crime that had raised the anger and anguish of a nation, peer pressure if nothing else would make the jurors vote the death penalty.

Darrow convinced the families of this and, in a move that came as a great surprise to the prosecutors, who had expected an insanity plea, pled Leopold and Loeb guilty. That way he would dispense with the jury and would only have to convince one man—the judge—not to hang two teenage boys. State's Attorney Crowe, furious at Darrow's unexpected move, insisted on presenting his whole case during what should have been a simple hearing to assess evidence "in mitigation and aggravation" of the crime. The people of Chicago were going to have their day in court, and Crowe made it clear that he wanted and expected the defendants to hang.

During the 32-day trial, the verdict of which was known on the first day, Crowe, at great length and in meticulous detail, tried the two boys. Darrow tried the death penalty. In his two-day summation, he went over the state's case, pointed out that no boys so young had ever been executed in Illinois, that few defendants that pled guilty had ever been sentenced to death, that the prosecution's thirst for blood was no more wholesome than the defendants'. Quoting poetry, and speaking of the progress of humanity, Darrow continued:

> I know, your honor, that ninety unfortunate human beings had been hanged by the neck until dead in the city of Chicago in our history. We would not have civilization except for those ninety that were hanged, and if we cannot make it ninety-two we shall have to shut up shop.
>
> . . . It might shock the fine sensibilities of the state's counsel that [Bobby Franks] was put into a culvert and left after he was dead, but, your honor, I can think of a scene that makes this pale into insignificance. I can think . . . of taking two boys, one eighteen and the other nineteen, irresponsible, weak, diseased; penning them up in a cell, checking off the days and the hours and the minutes, until they will be taken out and hanged. Wouldn't it be a glorious triumph for the State's Attorney? Wouldn't it be a glorious illustration for Christianity and kindness and charity? I can picture them, wakened in the gray light of morning, furnished a suit of clothes by the state, led to the scaffold, their feet tied, black caps drawn over their heads, stood on a trap-door, the hangman pressing a spring, so that it gives way under them; I can see them falling through space—and—stopped by the rope around their necks.

Crowe informed the court that he considered Darrow's belief that it was wrong to hang people so pernicious that "a greater blow has been struck to our institutions than by a hundred, yes a thousand murders." The judge deliberated for a week, informed Darrow that his eloquence had been wasted as he (the judge) was going to do what the law demanded, and then sentenced Leopold and Loeb to life imprisonment with a strong recommendation that they never be paroled.

The Evidence

Now was the time for Prosecutor Weiss to go over the evidence and decide what he was going to present, in what order, and how he would present it. His investigators were still gathering facts and searching for new witnesses, but the outline of the crime had gathered form and substance, and he pretty much knew what he was going to have to work with. He sat down and outlined his case:

• *Lucille Lane and J.J. Johansohn were having an affair, and had been for some time. Witnesses could put them together in various restaurants and social events over the past half year, starting well before Lucille Lane and Broderick Lane had separated. Johansohn was still living with his wife at the time of the murder, in a large house they jointly owned (Arkham is a community property state) in an exclusive suburb. This would explain why the lovers had their trysts in his office. Photographs of the office and its inner bedroom, or perhaps a visit by the jury, could establish its fitness for the purpose.*

• *Broderick Lane was unreasonably (we will not say insanely if we are the prosecution) jealous of his wife, and witnesses could testify that he had yelled at her several times and had struck her on at least one occasion for her supposed undue attentions to another man. This was one of the reasons she had left him. There was also some medical evidence that he had been abusive in a more physical way once or twice, but it might not be admissible.*

• *Broderick Lane had no intention of losing Lucille. At least one person would testify that he had said on one occasion: "If I can't have her, no one else will."*

• *Lucille Lane was filing for divorce. Broderick Lane had made it clear that he would fight her all the way. Weiss thought he could make a case that Lane had a pathological hatred of giving up any of his possessions and that he considered his wife a possession. Weiss also believed that Lucille almost certainly knew details of Broderick's business practices that could be used against him in a divorce proceeding, which would result in his having to give up many less animate possessions.*

- *Broderick Lane had hired private detectives, who had followed Lucille and J.J. to their trysting place and reported back to Lane. So he knew where they were and what they were doing.*

- *Broderick Lane claimed he was home in bed at the time of the murder, an unsubstantiated alibi.*

- *The victims were shot several times, indicating rage or frenzy, and nothing was stolen from the jewelry store. This was strongly indicative of a crime of passion.*

- *A witness saw a black Mercedes like the one owned by Broderick Lane leaving the alley behind the jewelry store at about 2:30 in the morning the night of the murder. He thought that the man behind the wheel was Broderick Lane.*

- *Traces of blood that were DNA-matched to Lucille Lane had been found on a pair of Broderick Lane's shoes.*

- *The murder weapon was a .28-caliber Fosdick-Hubbart revolver, a very rare handgun, identified by the characteristic marks left on the bullets. Broderick Lane had owned a .28-caliber Fosdick-Hubbart revolver but was unable to produce it, claiming that it had been stolen some time before. Investigators were trying to establish where he had been known to fire it, perhaps at a target range, to see if they could find some slugs to match with the bullets recovered from the victims.*

The chain of circumstantial evidence surrounding Broderick Lane looked tight to Weiss, but circumstantial evidence is no stronger than its weakest link. Weiss knew that if the defense could break the chain at any one point, it could all fall apart. Weiss would have to redouble his efforts to strengthen the links.

FOUR

THE PRE-TRIAL

> *Why may not that be the skull of a lawyer? Where be his quiddities now,*
> *his quillets, his cases, his tenures, and his tricks?*

— WILLIAM SHAKESPEARE
Hamlet, ACT V, SCENE 1

The trial of State of Arkham v Lane *was scheduled to begin in Department Four of the Superior Court, in and for the County of Metropolis, Judge Frances Merkle presiding, on May 12th, about eight months after the murders. This might not be your idea of a speedy trial, but it involved almost indecent haste.*

Major capital cases can take several years to come to trial as both sides investigate and gather evidence. The state must decide whether it is going for the death penalty, and the defense has to reveal whether it intends to use an insanity defense or any other strategy for which the state might need time to prepare. When the trial is about to begin, the attorneys for both sides meet with the judge beforehand to work out the ground rules regarding what evidence will be excluded and which of the expert witnesses for each side will be allowed to testify.

In the case at hand, State's Attorney Weiss would now turn over to Defense Attorney Porter a transcript of the grand jury testimony of any witness he knew he was going to call at the trial so that Porter would have a chance to study it for his cross-examination. Not all states are as progressive as this, but Arkham believes in making the playing field as even as possible for both sides.

Which is not to say that all traps are to be avoided. It is still permissible for each side to attempt to confuse and obfuscate, as long as they stay within the guidelines. Each side, for example, would be looking over the other's witness lists and wondering, "Why on earth is he calling him?" *And it could well be that a couple of the names were put on the list merely to make the opposition wonder, worry, and waste time investigating a witness that wasn't really going to be called.*

In the jockeying for position that will go on, Artemus Porter and Carter Weiss would be trying to outguess each other on such matters as whether obtaining a delay in the trial date would be more beneficial to the prosecution or the defense. Porter would be working under the disadvantage that his client was in jail awaiting the trial, as capital murder is not a bailable offense in Arkham, even for the rich and famous. But Porter was sure that Broderick Lane would rather be in jail for a little longer before the trial than in prison for a lot longer after.

In addition to the detectives continuing to investigate the case for the prosecution, Artemus Porter had his own investigators out working. Not only were they interviewing the prosecution's witnesses and seeking out new witnesses and evidence for the defense, they were also doing background investigations on everyone in the jury pool in order to give Porter some ammunition when he examined them in court.

DISCOVERY

"Discovery," the process of exchanging documents, witness lists, and other information with the opposite side in a court case before the start of trial, began for civil cases with the dawn of the twentieth century and slowly grew to be included in criminal cases. There was strong resistance to it from judges and lawyers who saw criminal trials as akin to trials-by-combat, jousting matches between the champions on each side, where God would guide the lance arm of the victor and thus truth and justice would prevail. Discovery in criminal cases was introduced in the federal courts in the 1940s, but it wasn't until the 1960s that it existed, in some form or other, in all the states.

In most states the burden of discovery in criminal cases is on the prosecution, which must reveal substantially all of its case without getting nearly as much in return. This allows the defendant to reserve his defense until he sees just what he has to defend against. But even the defense is supposed to reveal in a timely fashion some things on which the prosecution might reasonably be expected to need more information or might object to, such as an expert witness whose credentials the prosecution might want to check or documentary evidence that the prosecution might need to verify. A number of states have "Notice of Alibi" laws that require the defense to reveal any alibi it intends to introduce, along with the names of witnesses who will testify in support of that alibi.

THE COURTS

The word *court* derives from the Latin *curia*, the enclosed area in front of a house, a meaning it still maintains. It came to mean a place where people gather for a purpose, as in the royal court, or the tennis court. In legal parlance, a court is the location where a trial is held, the body holding the trial, and, narrowly, the presiding judge. Which is why "the court" can hand down a decision.

All courts in the United States are not created equal. There are four levels of courts in the federal judicial system and in that of most states.

The first, lowest-level courts in the state system are **courts of limited jurisdiction**, which try a variety of misdemeanors or minor violations. Their authority is limited by statute or judicial direction as to what sorts of cases they can try and what penalties they can assess. Some of these courts are quite specialized. They are presided over by justices of the peace, magistrates, or judges, who often fail to possess an extensive (or any) legal background, or even a law degree. Often state law does not require a jury trial for offenses tried in these courts. Among them, with names varying from state to state, are the:

Police Court
Justice Court
Magistrates Court
Municipal Court
District Court
Small Claims Court
Traffic Court
City Court
Juvenile Court
Housing Court

Some larger cities have Night Courts to take care of petty cases that arise during the evening hours. Four score years ago Los Angeles and

San Diego had Sunrise Courts, which met at 5:30 in the morning to handle the newly sober drunks arrested the night before.

The second level is made up of **courts of general jurisdiction.** The major workhorses of the judicial system, they try felony criminal cases, including murder, and civil matters ranging from disputes of a few thousand dollars to the breaking up of large corporations. These are generally cases in which the defendant may request a jury trial. The judges, whether appointed or elected, are generally experienced lawyers when they take office. In different states this court will be known as:

District Court
Circuit Court
Superior Court
Court of General Sessions
Court of Common Pleas

In New York state, for some reason, the court of general jurisdiction is the Supreme Court. And in some places it is the wonderfully named Court of Oyer and Terminer, a name taken from special courts convened by English kings when there was no time to wait for the regular judicial process.

The third level, which about half of the states don't use, is an intermediate appellate court called the **Court of Appeals** or **Superior Court.** In some states this function is filled by the appellate division of the state's supreme court. The function of these courts is to hear appeals and provide an additional judicial layer between the trial court and the state's supreme court. Since they are not usually deciding questions of fact, they operate without juries, but have three or more judges sitting on each case, and majority rules.

The highest state courts are called the **Court of Appeals, Supreme Court,** and **Supreme Judicial Court.** (The New York State Court of Appeals was, until late in the nineteenth century, called by the unfortunate name of the "Court of Errors.")

These are the courts of last resort within the state. The only place an appeal can be taken from here is to the United States Supreme Court.

The corresponding federal courts begin at the lowest level with **United States Commissioners,** who are judges with authority to try minor federal crimes and issue warrants. At the next level, where most federal cases are tried, are the **district courts.** There are 94 federal districts covering all the states—some of the larger states have more than one—and several of the territories. Above the district courts are the thirteen **circuit courts of appeal**, and above all federal and state courts is the **Supreme Court of the United States**, the ultimate authority on both civil and criminal law in this country. The Supreme Court derives its authority from the Constitution, and is its final interpreter.

The Sixth Amendment to The Constitution of the United States guarantees all criminal defendants "the right to a speedy and public trial." And indeed most poor defendants get trials that are altogether too speedy. It used to be a ploy of defense attorneys to delay the start of a trial for as long as possible, especially if the defendant was out on bail. After all, the longer the delay, the greater the chance that the state's key witnesses might die or move away, or simply fail to appear due to their boredom with coming to court time after time to discover that the trial has once more been postponed. Of course, the more important the trial, or the more prominent the defendant, the less the chance of this being an effective strategy.

One of the continuing complaints by those not involved in the criminal justice system is the time it sometimes takes to bring a defendant to trial. The public seems to equate a prolonged judicial process with justice denied, especially to the victims of the crime. But occasionally a defendant is innocent, and her counsel may need sufficient time to review the evidence and the witnesses to discover how to rebut. As trial attorney Louis Nizer put it:

> *A man's liberty is too precious to be sacrificed even on so noble an altar as that called "Prompt Enforcement." Anyone who is impatient with the law's delay (right as he is in many areas) would be more tolerant on this subject if ever he was unfortunate enough to be accused of violating one of the tens of thousands of statutes, and suddenly found his business undermined, his family distressed, his lifelong associations broken, and his entire life crumbling under the pressure of accusation. Such a man would not consider any safeguard provided by law too extreme or time-consuming. He would understand that the concern of the law for his reputation and liberty is balm in a desperate hour.* (The Jury Returns, 1966.)

So the defense attorney has to figure out just how much of an extension he needs to investigate the prosecution's witnesses for possible skeletons in their closets, while hoping that the prosecution will not discover that his chief character witness was arrested for stealing chickens in Omaha in 1956.

While having surprise witnesses is permitted, given a reasonable excuse ("We were just able to locate Mr. Lupoff, your honor."), it is a ploy of limited value. The other side can reasonably expect a delay in either the trial or in its cross-examination ("This comes as a complete surprise to us, your honor, and we will need a few days to prepare our cross-examination.").

DEFENSE TACTICS

Broderick Lane insisted that he was innocent, even to his own attorney. But that was not surprising; few of Artemus Porter's clients had admitted guilt. Which was a good thing, since he could then defend them in good conscience and in accord with the rules of the ethics committee of the Arkham Bar Association. Which was also a bad thing, since Porter always had to try to prepare for surprises from the prosecution, especially in the form of little facts that his client hoped no one would ever discover. Sometimes they were not connected to the crime but put his client in a bad light, were innocent actions that could be misinterpreted to indicate guilt, or were damning facts that would require all of Porter's forensic skills to neutralize. Whichever the case, he would rather hear about them first from his client than from a prosecution witness during the trial.

Lane claimed that he was nowhere near the crime scene on the night of the murder. But, just in case the prosecution could prove otherwise, Porter had to consider other possibilities. There are other ways to be innocent—or at least not guilty—than not having committed the crime, although even Broderick Porter would have a tough time making a jury believe them:

- **Accident:** *"Mr. Lane fired his pistol by accident, just happening to kill his wife and her lover."*
- **Duress:** *"A strange man forced my client at gunpoint to kill his wife and her lover."*
- **Self-Defense:** *"Mr. Lane's wife pulled a gun on him, and he killed her and her lover to save his own life. Then he thoughtlessly took her gun away with him."*
- **Intoxication:** *"Someone slipped a strange drug into my client's stew, which caused him to go crazy and kill his wife and her lover."*

The Insanity Defense

Now, if the prosecution looked as though it were able to place Lane at the crime scene, the one remaining possibility would be an insanity defense. The "unwritten law" about which so much has been written wouldn't help in this case. It supposedly applied when a spouse was caught in flagrante delicto *(which very loosely translates to "in the very act"). This gave the jury a reasonable excuse to find the defendant not guilty by reason of temporary insanity, but what they were really saying was "the so-and-so victim deserved it." But since juries often wouldn't go along with this argument and convicted anyway, it was a dangerous defense strategy. And when the husband and wife are separated, and have been for some time, as in the case of Broderick and Lillian Lane, and the husband has to follow his wife across town to catch her and her lover and presumably bring his weapons with him, the element of surprise is missing, and the word "temporary" would have to be stretched past the common understanding.*

But if Lane was convincingly placed at the scene of the crime by competent witnesses or evidence, and if he could be shown to have had a weapon like the one that killed the two victims, then a true insanity defense might be necessary. In any case, Porter would put a couple of high-priced psychiatrists on his witness list and schedule meetings with Lane for them. They might prove helpful. And, in any case, they would annoy the prosecution, always a worthwhile goal.

BY REASON OF INSANITY

On Friday, January 20, 1843, in a shot heard round the world, Scottish woodcutter and conspiracy theorist Daniel M'Naghten fired at and killed Edward Drummond, private secretary of Sir Robert Peel. M'Naghten was under the impression that he was shooting Sir Robert, then Prime Minister of Great Britain. He was further under the delusion that Sir Robert Peel, founder of the first London police force, was part of a cabal, along with the Pope and the Society of Jesus, that plotted to abridge the rights of British subjects and that had deliberately set out to spy on and persecute him.

That M'Naghten was insane there was no doubt; nine medical experts testified for the defense, and none for the prosecution. That insanity was accepted as a defense came as a surprise, and that M'Naghten was acquitted "by reason of insanity" came as a shock. A rhyming couplet expressed the popular opinion:

"Ye people of England exult and be glad
"For you're now at the will of the merciless mad!"

Her Majesty Queen Victoria was not amused. She feared that the acquittal would encourage future madmen to attack her other ministers or herself. The House of Lords, which doubles as England's highest deliberative body (the equivalent of our Senate) and highest judicial body (as is our Supreme Court), asked a panel of common law judges to examine the insanity plea. The judges reported that insanity was an allowable defense in medieval canon law, and that as early as the thirteenth century Henry III had pardoned murderers found to be insane. The earliest instance they could find of a jury accepting an insanity defense was in 1505.

The House of Lords debated what would constitute a valid insanity defense and in what circumstance a defendant should be allowed to plead that a mental defect absolved him from the guilt of his actions. Just as every defendant is presumed to be innocent, they decided, so is he presumed to be sane. Which means that, although the prosecution must prove him guilty to convict, the defense must prove him insane to use that as a defense. And further that

> . . . *to establish a defense on the grounds of insanity, it must be clearly proved that, at the time of the committing of the act, the party accused was laboring under such a defect of reason, from disease of the mind, as not to know the nature and quality of the act he was doing; or, if he did know it, that he did not know he was doing what was wrong.*[1]

This is the basis for what has become known as the M'Naghten Test or the Right-Wrong Test, the rule under which insanity defenses labored for the next hundred years. Under M'Naghten, the consideration of insane behavior, for the purposes of a criminal trial, came down to whether the accused knew the "nature and quality" of his act and whether he knew that the act was wrong. That is: if the defendant strangled the victim but was under the impression at the time that he was squeezing a lemon, then he is not guilty of murder, as he could not have plotted or even intended the act, being unaware that he was committing

---

1. Daniel M'Naghten Case, *10 C.F. 200, 210–211, 8 Eng. Rep. 718 722–723 (1843).*

it. If the defendant knew that he was strangling someone, but was unaware that it was wrong to do so, he is also not guilty. Let us say that he actively, although incorrectly, believed that the victim was plotting to kill him at the time, or that the victim was the devil newly released from Hell. Therefore, as he did not intend a crime, no crime was committed.

To this some American courts added another possibility: "irresistible impulse." This impulse was one that arose, as John F. Dillon, the Chief Justice of the Supreme Court of Iowa, put it in 1868, "not from natural passion, but from an insane condition of the mind." The theory was that if the defendant knew exactly what he was doing, and knew that it was wrong but was not in control of his own actions—if he could neither help himself nor stop himself from committing the crime—then he was not criminally at fault.

In 1869, New Hampshire went down the road less traveled and in *State v Pike* used the test simply to determine whether the crime was the "offspring or product of mental disease." Tests for this, according to Chief Justice Charles Doe's decision, were "purely questions of fact," and the jury was the decider of facts.

All of these decisions left the proving of the condition up to the defendant, and the insanity defense was seldom used and seldom successful when attempted. The most famous nineteenth-century case in America was the trial of Charles Julius Guiteau for the assassination of President James Garfield in the Baltimore & Potomac railroad station in Washington, D.C., on July 2, 1881. Guiteau was a truly insane religious fanatic who believed that Garfield should have appointed him ambassador to France. The judge allowed use of the M'Naghten test, but, despite Guiteau's professed belief that God had told him to kill Garfield, the jury refused to buy it. Guiteau was found guilty and was hanged on June 3, 1882. He went to the gallows singing a song he had written in prison which began with the words, "I am going to the Lordy."

Psychiatrists had never been happy with the M'Naghten test, as it didn't allow them to express the infinite subtle varieties of mental illness in their courtroom testimony. Neurosis, psychosis, paranoia, and schizophrenia, among others, were diagnoses a judge might allow psychiatrists to elaborate on during their testimonies to establish their credentials as men of science. The court, however, wanted only to establish whether the accused knew what he was doing, whether he knew it was wrong, and whether he was acting on an "irresistible impulse." Protesting that the term had no clinical meaning wouldn't help.

"Insane" to a trial court was a limited technical description, and the fact that it bore little relation to what psychiatrists considered mental illness as the twentieth century progressed was of no interest to the court.

In 1954, in *Durham v United States*, Court of Appeals Judge David Bazelon worked to amend the standard. In reversing the conviction of Monte Durham for housebreaking, Bazelon created what became known as the "Durham rule." He noted that Durham's history of mental problems had not been considered, and he felt that an accused should be able to plead an insanity defense "if his unlawful act was the product of mental disease or mental defect." This effectively put the onus of proof in the lap of the prosecution. The defendant could claim that a mental defect had caused him to commit the crime, then find one or two captive psychiatrists to define the defect, causing the prosecution to have to martial a battalion of experts to disprove it.

This was quickly found to be an unsatisfactory situation, since the new rule merely confused both court and jury. In 1972, in *United States v Brawner*, the Court of Appeals threw out the Durham Rule and adopted the standard, used by many states today, that was developed for the Model Penal Code of the American Law Institute. This standard, known as the A.L.I. test or the Brawner rule, would deem a defendant not guilty by reason of insanity if, at the time of the offense, "as a result of mental disease or defect he lacks substantial capacity either to appreciate the criminality of his conduct or to conform his conduct to the requirements of law."

In 1974, Judge Bazelon commented on the failure of Durham: "My experience has shown that in no case is it more difficult to elicit productive and reliable expert testimony than in cases that call on the knowledge and practice of psychiatry."

In a move that seems to be spreading, and that so far has affected about a dozen states, another possible verdict has been added to the list: guilty but insane. This is for defendants who are judged sane enough to have known what they were doing, and to have been able to control themselves, and thus should receive punishment for their crime, but are perceived to be insane enough that their mental state should be considered as a mitigating circumstance.

In some states this has resulted in a bifurcated trial, consisting of, first, a hearing to determine the accused's guilt or innocence, and then, if found guilty, a second hearing before the same jury to determine his sanity. This has put some lawyers in the interesting position of working to prove that their client did not commit the crime, and then in an elaborate slight-of-mind working to prove that, although he did commit it, he was crazy at the time.

During this past century the insanity defense has been used in a number of high-profile trials, with mixed results.

—On January 6, 1908, Harry Kendall Thaw went on trial for the second time for the murder of Stanford White, an architect who had designed several of New York City's more important buildings, including the original Madison Square Garden, where he was killed. Thaw had married Evelyn Nesbit, a beautiful showgirl, and then became obsessed to the point of lunacy over the fact that she had previously had an affair with White. On June 25, 1906, Thaw shot White several times in the back of the head while White was seated at the opening performance of *Mam'zelle Champagne*, a stage show, in the terrace garden of Madison Square Garden. Thaw immediately surrendered to a uniformed fireman who was standing by the exit, explaining, "He ruined my life," or possibly, "He ruined my wife."

Delphin Delmas, a flamboyant trial lawyer, represented Thaw. He asserted that Thaw, enraged by White's seduction of his wife—although it happened before Thaw met his wife—had killed him in a momentary passion. This meant that, although he was insane at the moment of the murder, the rage had passed and he was no longer insane. This plea of temporary insanity, now a staple device of defense attorneys, was novel when Delmas used it. The prosecution admitted that Thaw was strange, and probably paranoid, but insisted that he knew what he was doing, and that the act he committed was a plain old murder for jealousy.

The first jury was hopelessly deadlocked. Thaw was retried, and the second jury found him "not guilty because of insanity at the time of the act." He was locked up at the New York State Asylum for the Criminally Insane at Mattewan. In 1915 he was released as recovered. Two years later he was convicted of horsewhipping a boy and was recommitted to the asylum, where he remained until 1924.

—David Berkowitz, the notorious "Son of Sam" killer, terrorized New York City in 1976 by shooting people—usually amorous couples in parked cars—with a .44-caliber handgun. He killed six people and seriously wounded seven before he was caught. Reviewing his history of psychopathic behavior and his insistence that he was getting his murderous instructions from a 2,000-year-old man named Sam, transmitted through the howling of dogs, a panel of psychiatrists found him incompetent to stand trial by reason of insanity but then reversed their decision when they decided he had been deluding them. He was still insane, they decided, but not insane enough to avoid trial. Berkowitz pled guilty. The judge questioned him to make sure he understood the plea, and asked him whether he had intended to cause serious injury to two of the women he had wounded. "Oh no, sir. I wanted to kill them," Berkowitz told the judge. He was sentenced to 25 years to life for each of the murders.

—On November 27, 1978, former city supervisor Dan White crawled through a basement window into San Francisco's city hall in order to avoid metal detectors at the doors and shot and killed Mayor George Moscone after a bitter argument. He then gratuitously hunted down Harvey Milk, San Francisco's first openly gay city supervisor, in another part of the building and shot him to death. White was a former fireman, a former policeman, and an extreme homophobe.

Unable to dispute the facts of the case, White's lawyer, Douglas Schmidt, settled on the defense that White was a severe manic depressive deep into his mania when he committed the crime. It was not first-degree murder, Schmidt averred, in spite of White's entry through a basement window and his hunting for Milk to kill him, because White was in the grips of an "irresistible impulse" at the time. In a classic attempt to try the victim for the crime, he contrasted White's he-man background with Milk's gay lifestyle. In what became known as the "Twinkie defense," he attributed White's mania to high blood sugar caused by junk food.

The jury found White guilty of two counts of voluntary manslaughter, showing that, against all logic, they chose to believe the irresistible impulse theory. Dan White was sentenced to the maximum of seven years and eight months in prison. He was paroled in 1984 and committed suicide in his garage in 1985.

—On March 30, 1981, as President Ronald Reagan was returning to the presidential limousine after giving a speech at Washington's

Hilton Hotel, 25-year-old John Hinckley, Jr. emptied his .22-caliber revolver at the president. Hinckley hit Reagan, Press Secretary James Brady, Secret Service agent Timothy J. McCarthy, and District of Columbia police officer Thomas Delahanty. None were killed, although James Brady suffered permanent severe motor impairment.

Hinckley, the son of an oil executive, grew up in Dallas, Texas, moving to Colorado in 1974 with his family. He attended Texas Tech, but never graduated; he joined the American Nazi Party, but was dropped from their membership because of his "violent nature." A letter found in his hotel room showed that he had a fixation on Jodie Foster, the Academy Award–winning actress who was a student at Yale at the time. The assassination was an attempt to win Ms. Foster's favor, an idea with which Hinckley had grown obsessed since he saw her in the movie *Taxi Driver.*

The prosecution showed how Hinckley had stalked the president and calmly and deliberately emptied his gun at his victim. Neurotic or not, they said, he knew what he was doing and the consequences of his act. His motive, a prosecution psychiatrist asserted, was instant fame. The defense told of his long-term fixation on Jodie Foster and showed a history of obsessive behavior that had placed Hinckley under the care of a psychiatrist.

Much to the surprise of the judge and the observers in the courtroom, and the disgust of the public, the jury returned a verdict of not guilty by reason of insanity. Instead of prison, Hinckley was sent to St. Elizabeth's Mental Hospital, where he still resides.

There is a general feeling among that part of the public that concerns itself with such matters that the insanity defense is a contrivance a clever defense attorney uses to free a guilty defendant. This feeling emerges with particular force right after a celebrated trial in which a defendant has been declared "not guilty by reason of insanity" by a jury. The truth is that the insanity defense is seldom used, and even more seldom accepted by the jury. And when a jury finds a defendant insane, he or she usually *is* insane. Harry Kendall Thaw and David Berkowitz were clearly crazy when they committed their crimes. Even Dan White was probably mentally unbalanced, as is indicated by his subsequent suicide.

It has been argued that any person who deliberately kills another for any reason other than defense of self, loved ones, or property is committing an insane act. But that is an ideal that our society has not yet reached. There are those who kill for gain, whose only defect is insufficient regard for human life. Some of those are sociopaths who do not think of other humans as real beings, but regard them as objects to be manipulated. For these people, murder becomes a final manipulation. Some others are moral imbeciles who regard life as a series of opportunities to "get away" with something. These people suffer from a mental defect, but it is not what the law defines as insanity.

On the other hand there are people who, due to a peculiar set of circumstances that probably would never arise again, find themselves murderers. This would include people who kill blackmailers, women who kill men who abuse them, and men who seek out and kill the ravishers of their wives, sisters, or daughters. If you walk into your house to find your wife being raped and shoot and kill the rapist, the chances of your even being indicted for any crime are slight. But if you go to get your gun and chase the rapist down the street and kill him two blocks away, you have committed murder, and you will probably be tried.

MOTIONS AND STIPULATIONS

Porter now went to a meeting with Weiss and Judge Merkle in the judge's chambers to discuss and agree to the various facts to which each party would stipulate before the case began. In this case both sides agreed:
- *that two human beings are dead;*
- *that their names were J.J. Johansohn and Lucille Lane; and*
- *that the killings occurred in the city of Metropolis, in the state of Arkham.*

• • •

In any criminal case, the prosecution must show that a crime has been committed before going any further. It is necessary in a murder trial for the prosecution to show that a human being was killed, that the death was the result of a criminal act, and that the killing occurred within the jurisdiction of the court before the prosecution can get down to trying to prove that the defendant committed the crime. This is known as the *corpus delicti*, which is Latin for "the body of the crime." The phrase is often misused to mean the body of the victim, but it refers to the physical proof that a crime has been committed. In a murder case, the victim's body is part of the proof—perhaps the most important part—but people have been convicted of murder without the body ever being found. It is not common, but it has happened.

Often much of the *corpus delicti*, the basic elements of the crime, will be stipulated to if they are not in dispute. A stipulation is a fact that is agreed upon by both sides, and thus is to be accepted by the jury without further proof. Its purpose is to save the court's time and the jury's patience. Stipulations may occur before or during the trial. When an expert witness takes the stand, for example, the opposing attorney might say, "I will stipulate that Dr. Maven qualifies as an expert in the field of phrenology." She can still cross-examine Dr. Maven about abstruse points of phrenological doctrine, but, having stipulated Dr. Maven's expertise, she can't cross-examine the phrenologist as to the validity of his credentials.

* * *

Judge Merkle informed the two attorneys that she had served on several committees with Broderick Lane, and so knew him slightly. She assured them that she had no other relationship with the defendant, and that she had no particular feelings of comradeship or of dislike for Lane and could certainly conduct the trial in a fair and impartial manner. But she offered to recuse herself if either side requested it. Both Weiss and Porter hastened to assure Judge Merkle that they were pleased to have her on the bench and desired no change.

Both sides also had several pre-trial motions and responses for the judge to consider. The defense filed a motion for a change of venue, wanting to move the case to Smallville, across the state, claiming that the great amount of publicity generated by the case made a fair trial impossible in Metropolis. The prosecution filed a response describing the people of Metropolis as the most fair-minded in the world and the publicity as negligible. The defense also filed a motion to suppress evidence regarding Broderick Lane's prior abuse of his wife, claiming that it didn't pertain to this trial and would unduly prejudice the jury. The prosecution responded that it went toward state of mind and was part of the motive. The defense further filed a motion to suppress the blood evidence, since DNA analysis was not yet reliable enough for courtroom use and the jury would not be able to properly weigh what it was told. The prosecution responded that DNA analysis was rapidly becoming as respectable in the forensic community as fingerprint typing, and they would be glad to argue its reliability before the jury.

The judge took these motions under advisement and promised to hold hearings on them before the trial began.

• • •

The judge establishes the rules by which each case will be tried, and most are set by statute or precedent, such as the size of the jury; the order in which the parties present their cases—first prosecution, then defense; and the definition of the crime itself. But because each case is unique, each presents problems in the definition or application of these rules. The judge's impartiality must be beyond question. If the judge is the defendant's brother-in-law, he should recuse himself (remove himself from the case). But if the judge's only connection with the defendant was that he once sat in the same room with the defendant at a dinner, he would probably retain his neutrality unless the defendant spilled a bowl of hot soup in his lap.

There is such a thing as too much pre-trial publicity, but at just what point is this line crossed? There are new scientific techniques that are not yet acceptable as evidence in a courtroom. In the past, some, like fingerprinting, gained rapid acceptance. Others, like polygraphs ("lie detectors"), have yet to be accepted as reliable in most courtrooms. At what point does a particular test have enough respectability to be used? The consensus is that when the test has gained common acceptance in the scientific community as being valid it can be used. It is up to the judge to decide when this nebulous point has been reached.

The attorneys on each side try to help the judge reach these decisions with their motions, which are offered before the trial. In some cases, new motions are introduced during the trial until the jury returns a verdict. At that time, if the verdict was unfavorable to the defense, the defense attorney would transfer his attentions to the appeals court.

When a change of venue is requested or a question arises about the admissability of scientific evidence, hearings are usually held, without the jury present, so that experts for each side can testify on these issues.

THE PEOPLE'S RESPONSE

During the second trial of Erik and Lyle Menendez for the murder of their parents, the defense filed a 12-page motion to exclude evidence of the brothers' spending after the murders on grounds that "the proffered evidence is irrelevant, or, if marginally relevant, its probative value is substantially outweighed by the probability that its admission will necessitate undue consumption of time or create substantial danger of undue prejudice, or of confusing the issues and of misleading the jury."

The prosecution, which maintained that the brothers murdered their parents at least partly for money, filed this response, which goes over much of the defense's motion in attempting to refute it:

1	GIL GARCETTI District Attorney
	DAVID P. CONN Head Deputy District Attorney
2	CAROL JANE NAJERA Deputy District Attorney
	210 West Temple Street
3	Los Angeles, California 90012
	Attorneys for Plaintiff
4	Original Filed June 19, 1995 Los Angeles Superior Court
5	
6	SUPERIOR COURT OF THE STATE OF CALIFORNIA,
7	IN AND FOR THE COURT OF LOS ANGELES

8		
9	PEOPLE OF THE STATE OF CALIFORNIA, Plaintiff	Case No. BA068880 DATE: June 26, 1995 TIME: 9:00 A.M.
10	v	PLACE: Department NW, "N"
11		PEOPLE'S RESPONSE
12	JOSEPH LYLE MENENDEZ and ERIK GALEN MENENDEZ,	MOTION TO EXCLUDE DEFENDANT'S'
13	Defendants	EVIDENCE OF SPENDING
14		
15		
16	TO THE HONORABLE STANLEY WEISBERG, JUDGE OF THE	
17	VAN NUYS SUPERIOR COURT, and TO THE DEFENDANTS AND	
18	THEIR ATTORNEYS:	

PLEASE TAKE NOTICE that on June 26, 1995, the People of the State of California will oppose the defendants' motion entitled "MOTION IN LIMINE RE RECENTLY PROFFERED SPENDING EVIDENCE." This opposition will be based upon this notice, the attached points and authorities, and such argument as will be made at the time of the hearing of the motion.

INTRODUCTION

This court has previously ruled that the prosecution may present evidence that after the defendants murdered their parents, they spent their parents' money. This evidence includes the following purchases and attempted purchases:

1. Two Rolex watches and money clips (Both defendants)

2. Marina City Condominium (Both defendants)

3. Porsche (Lyle Menendez)

4. Clothing and accessories—New Jersey and New York (Lyle Menendez)

5. A Private limousine and body guard—New Jersey and New York (Lyle Menendez)

6. A patio home (Lyle Menendez)

7. A townhouse (Lyle Menendez)

8. A restaurant—Chuck's Spring Street Cafe (Lyle Menendez)

9. A million-dollar-plus residence in Newport Beach (Erik Menendez)

10. A Jeep Wrangler (Erik Menendez)

11. A private tennis coach (Erik Menendez)

12. A pool table (Erik Menendez)

With the exception of the million-dollar-plus residence in Newport Beach, all of the above-cited spending evidence was ruled admissible in some form in the first trial. This Court has since ruled it admissible in a joint trial conducted before a single jury. The defendants now seek to exclude additional evidence of their spending.

Specifically, they seek to exclude evidence of the following expenditures:

1. Rental of the bungalow suite at the Hotel Bel-Aire

2. A ski trip to Aspen

3. Clothing and accessories purchased in Chicago, Illinois

4. A private limousine used in Beverly Hills and Chicago, Illinois

5. A Sony Big Screen entertainment center

6. A Saab automobile

7. A vacation to Cancun, Mexico

8. Skiing and gambling in Lake Tahoe

9. Traveling the professional tennis circuit

10. Investments at Smith Barney

The Defendants argue that insofar as the People can demonstrate that each defendant fraudulently obtained $350,000 from the insurance company, the prosecution should be precluded from also presenting evidence that they spent the money obtained. They argue that evidence of spending

1 is more prejudicial than probative, and that it is inadmissible character evi-

2 dence.

3   Similar objections, made under Evidence Code 352 and 1101, were

4 argued on June 17 and July 26, 1993, before the start of the first trial. At

5 that time the court ruled that such evidence is not inadmissible character

6 evidence. The court also evaluated the evidence under Evidence Code

7 Section 352, and determined that the probative value of the evidence out-

8 weighed any possible prejudice to the defendants.

9   Similar objections were raised after the first trial. On April 3, 1995

10 this court once again evaluated evidence of spending under Evidence Code

11 Section 352 and found it admissible. Additional arguments to exclude evi-

12 dence of spending were made on April 4, 1995, and were rejected by the

13 court.

14   The Court has thus considered and discussed, at length, the very issues

15 raised by the defendants in this motion in regard to evidence of spending,

16 and the court has repeatedly ruled that the defendants' arguments are with-

17 out merit.

18   The defendants seek to exclude all but one of the following 13 areas

19 of evidence which the People seek to present to the jury.

20   1. The party at the Hotel Bel-Aire—In the first trial, spending at the

21 Hotel Bel-Aire was excluded after the defendants presented the testimony of

22 their cousin Henry Llanio, who testified that he helped select the accom-

23 modations at the hotel as a meeting place for the family immediately after

24 the murders, and that he assumed the bill would be paid by LIVE

25 Entertainment.

26   In fact, the People will show through the testimony of Robin

Rosenbloom and others that the defendants used the suite to entertain their friends, and that they threw a party immediately after the memorial service in which, in the words of Ms. Rosenbloom, "no adults" were in attendance. The defendants rented the most expensive suite, ordered caviar and champagne, and Lyle Menendez paid for the accommodations.

The People seek to present evidence of the lavish accommodations available to them following the murders of their parents, as well as the use they made of such accommodations. This evidence is relevant to their state of mind immediately after the murder of their parents, and is circumstantial evidence of their state of mind at the time of the murder of their parents.

2. The Aspen ski trip—Testimony will show that the defendants took a vacation shortly after they killed their parents. The issues raised by the defendants in their response in regard to this evidence are matters which may be the proper subject of cross-examination, but such matters do not go to the admissibility of the evidence.

3. Shopping in Chicago, Illinois—This evidence of spending is similar to the evidence of spending already ruled admissible by this court through the testimony of Richard Wenskowski and Glenn Stevens. Here again, issues raised by the defendants in their response in regard to this evidence are matters which may be the proper subject of cross-examination, but such matters do not go to the admissibility of the evidence.

4. Limousine rentals in Beverly Hills—The rental of limousine for personal transportation is similar to the evidence previously ruled admissible through the testimony of Richard Wenskowski. This evidence is admissible for the same reason that limousine rentals in New Jersey and New York were ruled admissible in the first trial.

5. Limousine rentals in New Jersey—Lyle Menendez' rental of limousines was ruled admissible in the first trial, and should be ruled admissible once again. Also admissible is Lyle Menendez' interest in pricing bullet-proof limousines.

6. Limousine rentals in New York—Lyle Menendez' limousine rental in New York was ruled admissible in the first trial, and should be found to be admissible once again.

7. Limousine rentals in Chicago, Illinois—This evidence is admissible for the same reason that limousine rentals in New Jersey and New York were ruled admissible in the first trial.

8. The Sony Entertainment System—The People have provided the defendants with a statement by Perry Berman in which he discusses his personal observations and knowledge of a purchase of an elaborate and expensive Sony sound system by Lyle Menendez. The defendants argue that this purchase cannot be proven without documentation. While documentation may be one way to establish the purchase, the testimony of a witness having personal knowledge of this matter is an equally valid way to establish the disputed fact.

9. A Saab automobile—Lyle Menendez' purchase of a vehicle for Jamie Pisarcik is relevant and admissible to show the defendant's use of his ill-begotten gain. This evidence is not challenged by the defendants.

10. The Cancun, Mexico vacation—Here again the defendants offer no proper reason why this evidence should be ruled inadmissible. Here again also, documentation is not the only way to establish the expenditures of the defendant, and the testimony of a percipient witness can establish this fact. Nor is it relevant that the parents of the defendants took the defendants on

similar vacations before the defendants killed them. That the defendants may have been accustomed to living well does not defeat evidence of motive; to the contrary, it demonstrates what the defendants were afraid of losing if they were to be cut out of the will. For that reason, it establishes motive all the more.

11. The Lake Tahoe ski trip—Evidence of a vacation and gambling, in Lake Tahoe, including the fact that the defendant borrowed money from Mark Slotkin is additional evidence of the defendant's state of mind, and there is no proper reason to exclude it.

12. Professional tennis circuit—Israel—The defendant argues that this is evidence of "work,"—an argument to which only the privileged could relate. In truth, this is evidence of the defendant's pursuit of his personal goal of becoming a professional tennis player, a pursuit made possible with the blood money of his dead parents.

13. Investments at Smith-Barney Florida—This evidence of Erik Menendez' spending is comparable to the purchase of a restaurant by Lyle Menendez and should be ruled admissible on the same basis. Both are relevant to the defendants' motive for committing the murders.

CONCLUSION

The defendants object to the admission of all but one of the 13 items of evidence discussed above. Only two of these items were ruled admissible in the first trial; the other items were not offered. The defendants argue that one item of evidence was previously ruled inadmissible (the spending at the Hotel Bel-Aire) but the People ask that this evidence be admitted based

1   upon the evidence and arguments only now advanced by the prosecution in

2   regard to this evidence.

3   The defendants request that this court exclude evidence of spending

4   pursuant to Evidence Codes sections 350, 352 and 1101. In light of the pre-

5   vious rejection by this court of similar arguments advanced in regard to sim-

6   ilar items of evidence, the People respectfully ask that this court deny the

7   defendants' request.

8

9   Respectfully submitted this 19th day of June 1995
        /s/ David P. Conn
        /s/ Carol J. Najera

With the preliminaries over, and each side in the best legal and factual position that the law and the judge allows, the trial begins.

FIVE

THE TRIAL BEGINS

> *In all criminal prosecutions, the accused shall enjoy the right to a speedy and public trial, by an impartial jury of the State and district wherein the crime shall have been committed, which district shall have been previously ascertained by law, and to be informed of the nature and cause of the accusation; to be confronted with the witnesses against him; to have compulsory process for obtaining witnesses in his favor, and to have the Assistance of Counsel for his defense.*
>
> —— CONSTITUTION OF THE UNITED STATES, AMENDMENT VI, 1791.

In his book *Courts and Criminals*, first published in 1909, Arthur Train, a prosecutor in New York City, wrote:

> A murder trial is the most solemn proceeding known to the law. [The writer] has prosecuted at least fifty men for murder, and convicted more than he cares to remember. Such trials are invariably dignified and deliberate so far as the conduct of the legal side of the case is concerned. No judge, however unqualified for the bench; no prosecutor, however light-minded; no lawyer, however callous, fails to feel the serious nature of the transaction or to be affected strongly by the fact that he is dealing with life and death. A prosecutor who openly laughed or sneered at a prisoner charged with murder would severely injure his case. The jury, naturally, is overwhelmed with the gravity of the occasion and the responsibility resting upon them.

In Train's time, these sentiments were basically accurate. It is only during this century that the murder trial as circus has become an established institution. Part of this may be attributed to the growth of the popular press, with each newspaper striving to attract a larger and larger readership with more and more sensational stories. Then came radio, bringing live coverage of sensational trials, and television with its visual impact and its nationwide, or worldwide, audience. There has been much criticism of bringing the camera into the courtroom, but a courtroom is a comparatively sedate and organized venue. Most of the problems of sensationalism, I think, are caused by cameras outside the courtroom: emotional interviews with the relatives of the victims; the spreading of unsubstantiated rumors; and interviews with supposed witnesses giving testimony to millions of viewers, witnesses who would not be allowed in the courtroom, or who at least would be subject to searching cross-examination. Highly sensational cases still make for bad trials, a problem for which no effective remedy has yet been found.

TRIALS OF THE CENTURY

—The first "Trial of the Century" of the twentieth century was the 1908 Thaw Trial, discussed on page 65. The second was the 1921 trial of Nicola Sacco and Bartolomeo Vanzetti for a murder committed during a robbery. The two men, one a fish peddler and the other a shoemaker, almost certainly committed neither the robbery nor the murder. They were anarchists, which is to say they believed that the least government possible was the best government. Today we would call them Republicans, but at that time they were identified with Communists and other allegedly dangerous radical thinkers. A "Red Scare" was going on after the recent ascension of Communism in Russia, and the Attorney General of the United States was busy rounding up Communists, anarchists, and other radicals by the thousands and deporting them. Many of them had to be readmitted to the country when it was pointed out that they were citizens by birth.

The evidence against the two anarchists was weak, and much of it was later shown to be mistaken or manufactured. Additionally, much of the state's testimony was perjured. "[T]he case against Sacco and Vanzetti for murder," according to an analysis done by Felix Frankfurter, then a Harvard Law School professor, later a United States Supreme Court Justice, "was part of a collusive effort between the

District Attorney and agents of the Department of Justice to rid the country of these Italians because of their Red activities."

There were widespread protests both for and against Sacco and Vanzetti, with demonstrations spreading across the United States and reaching major cities in Europe and South America. The two were found guilty and sentenced to death. The protests went on, but Judge Webster Thayer, who had been heard out of court referring to the two defendants as "them Dago sons of bitches," denied all requests for a new trial. On August 23, 1927, Sacco and Vanzetti were electrocuted. "Did you see what I did to those anarchist bastards?" Judge Thayer asked a friend.

—The Leopold and Loeb hearing in 1924 was, strictly speaking, not a trial at all but a "hearing in mitigation and aggravation of the offense" of the two teenagers, who had already pled guilty. As there would be no jury, a row of telegraph machines with operators had been installed in the jury box. There were 200 seats in the courtroom reserved for the press and 600 newsmen and correspondents vying for them. Mobs of people fought for the 70 seats that had been allocated to the general public. Much to the surprise of the *Chicago Tribune,* which had offered to broadcast the trial over radio station WGN if the citizens of Chicago wished it, the final vote was 6,529 to 4,169 against the notion—probably the last time that good taste has won out over sensationalism at a major trial. As Hal Higdon records:

> The newspaper, however, did urge two reforms "to safeguard American justice": drastic restriction of pretrial publicity, coupled with full publicity during trials, which would include radio coverage. Admitting its "share of the blame," the paper observed that pretrial publicity had "become an abomination." Stimulated by public demand, the human craving for excitement, newspapers had for years engaged in an orgy of sensationalism and "journalistic lynch law."[1]

—The 1935 trial of Bruno Richard Hauptmann for the kidnapping and murder of Charles Lindbergh's baby was conducted in a surreal atmosphere of carnival madness and comprehensive prejudice against the defendant. Stanley Walker described it as:

---

1. *Hal Higdon,* The Crime of the Century.

. . . so spectacular, so bizarre, that in retrospect it seems almost incredible that things could have happened as they did. Everything conspired to make the trial dramatic. In its bare, simple outlines the case had all the ingredients of a starkly realistic mystery story. But that was not enough. It remained for the press, the radio, the officials and the spectators to make of it a fantastic extravaganza.[2]

Hauptmann was found guilty—no other decision was possible considering the hysteria surrounding the trial—and was sentenced to die in the electric chair. A persuasive case can be made that he was not guilty, and that whoever was guilty didn't work alone. Hauptmann was found in possession of some of the ransom money, which was the only bit of real evidence against him, yet the person who turned over the ransom money to a man in a graveyard at midnight described the recipient, and that description did not in the least resemble Hauptmann. It is also possible that whoever collected the ransom was not the one who kidnapped the Lindbergh baby, and the two sets of people might not have known each other. It is not clear that the decomposed body of a baby found in the New Jersey woods was that of the Lindbergh child, and the baby's own doctor believed it was not. The rest of the ransom money has never been found. The governor of New Jersey visited the condemned man secretly and stated that he had serious doubts about Hauptmann's guilt. He granted Hauptmann a 30-day reprieve for the Court of Pardons to examine the case. The court turned Hauptmann down, and the governor, by state law, had no further say in the matter. Hauptmann was executed on April 3, 1936.

—The 1951 trial of Julius and Ethel Rosenberg, who were charged with conspiracy to commit espionage in wartime, happened at a time when anti-Soviet hysteria was at its peak. The Soviet Union had the Atom bomb, schoolchildren were being taught to hide under desks, and it was portrayed as the Rosenbergs' fault. There was great doubt in large segments of the public as to their guilt, but a greater desire in the government and the masses to find someone to blame prevailed. Scapegoats were needed, and the Rosenbergs were convicted and executed. Recent documents uncovered in Soviet archives indicate that the Rosenbergs probably did spy, but even so, their execution in peacetime

2. *Stanley Walker*, Mrs. Astor's Horse.

for spying for a country that was an ally at the time was and remains unprecedented.

—In Cleveland in 1954, Dr. Sam Sheppard was tried for murder. Sheppard claimed that someone had entered his house late at night, knocked him unconscious, and savagely beaten his wife, Marilyn, to death. The prosecution insisted that he had done it himself. Prior to the trial there had been

> . . . three and one-half months of a vicious, all-permeating propaganda buildup against Sam and his family. It had been spontaneous, but the local newspapers, the television and radio stations, public officials, and citizens generally had taken part in it. No rational thought on the subject of Sam's guilt or innocence was possible any more. The large and vocal group of residents—perhaps a majority—who had come to accept Sam's guilt as a sort of axiom which needed no proof amounted to a mob loose in the community, an ominous, ugly mob intent on seeing to it that this man should not escape.[3]

Sheppard was found guilty on evidence that in no way contradicted his own story. The fact that Sheppard was having an affair with a lab assistant at his hospital was all the motive the jury needed. As for opportunity, well, he was in the house. As for means, no weapon had been found, but the county coroner testified that a bloodstain on the pillow corresponded to "a two-bladed surgical instrument with teeth on the end of each blade." The word *surgical* did its prejudicial work despite the fact that no "surgical instrument" of that description could be found in the catalogues of any surgical supply house. Sheppard was sentenced to life in prison.

It wasn't until 1965 that Sheppard's new attorney, a young F. Lee Bailey, managed to get the conviction set aside, citing numerous irregularities and mistakes including the fact that during the course of the trial the judge had acted in a manner obviously favoring the prosecution. Bailey discovered that early in the trial the judge had told a reporter, "Sheppard is guilty as hell." At the second trial in 1966, twelve years after his first conviction, with much publicity but a lot less passion, the jury took less than 12 hours to find Sheppard innocent.

---

3. *Paul Holmes,* The Sheppard Murder Case.

Other examples of trials where overwhelming public interest, public hysteria, or the misuse of governmental powers for political ends has diverted the course of justice include the Leo Franks trial in 1913; the Joe Hill trial in 1914; the trial of Tom Mooney in 1917; the trials of Roscoe "Fatty" Arbuckle in 1921 and 1922; the trial of Henry and William Stevens and Frances Hall in 1926 in the Hall-Mills murder case of 1922; the trial of the nine Scottsboro boys in 1931, with a series of additional trials until 1937; and the trial of Patty Hearst in 1976.

THE JURY

"Please rise," the bailiff said.

Everyone in the courtroom stood up as the judge, a small woman with large black-rimmed glasses, scurried into the room, her black robe fluttering behind her, and took her place in the judge's chair, a large, ornate, leather chair on the raised dais in front of the courtroom called the "bench." She nodded to the bailiff.

"Hear ye, hear ye, hear ye, the Court of General Sessions for the State of Arkham in and for the City and County of Metropolis is now in session, the Honorable Judge Frances Merkle presiding," the bailiff intoned, running the words together so fast that it was almost impossible to understand him. "All having business before this court come forth, give your attention and you shall be heard. God save the United States, the State of Arkham and this Honorable Court. Please be seated."

To the judge's left and lower down was the witness box. To the judge's right at floor level was the small enclosed area where the court clerk sat and kept track of everything that was happening. At a small table in front of the judge sat the court recorder, keeping a record of everything said "before the bar," that is, in the area in front of the railing separating the "actors" in this courtroom drama from the "specta-tors." To the far left of the judge, along the wall, was the jury box, consisting of two rows of chairs surrounded by a railing. Two long tables faced the bench. At one sat prosecutor Weiss and his assistants. At the other sat the defendant, Broderick Lane, his attorney, and a woman with oversized black-framed glasses and a notebook computer.

"In the matter of the State of Arkham versus Broderick Lane," the clerk called out, "the charge being two counts of murder in the first degree with special circum-stances. A plea of not guilty has been entered."

"Are we ready?" Judge Merkle asked, looking from one table to the other.

The people at both tables stood up. "Ready for the prosecution, your honor," Prosecutor Weiss said.

"Ready for the defense," attorney Porter declared.

"Good," the judge said. "Let's impanel a jury and get underway."

• • •

In the Constitution of the United States, and in 46 of the state constitutions, the right to a jury trial is guaranteed in all criminal cases. "Criminal cases" is usually interpreted to mean felonies, and juries are not deemed necessary in traffic court or night court or, in many states, in disposing of misdemeanor cases. The lists of those eligible to serve on a jury are drawn up in a variety of ways in different jurisdictions. Some places use voter registration, some driver's license records, some get the names from the local phone book, and some may use a combination of these and other sources.

Many lawyers consider picking the jury to be the single most important element toward winning their case. There are many myths surrounding jury selection: people of Mediterranean descent are believed to be emotional, and should be picked if you want to invoke the jury's anger or pity. People of Scandinavian stock are considered coldly rational, and should be chosen if the facts are on your side but the feeling is not. Older people are supposedly more indulgent. Men with facial hair are perceived as undependable. Writers, editors, and publishers are believed too intelligent, artists too romantic and imaginative. Butchers, according to myth, cannot be trusted to bring in a guilty verdict in a homicide case. Female jurors are expected to be harder on a female defendant than male jurors. Each trial lawyer brings to her juror selection process the superstitions and prejudices she has picked up in her years of practice. Most attorneys will admit that there is no rational basis for any of these feelings and that they may well be invalid. But, after all, why take a chance?

TRIAL BY JURY

Judging guilt or innocence and fixing punishment by committee is an ancient and widespread practice. Its advantages are clear: it serves to dilute responsibility and reinforce the justice of a decision.

In Athens around the fourth century B.C. there was a form of jury trial that we'd find undesirable and hard to imitate. Six thousand jurors called *dikasts,* were picked by lot each year from among the male citizens over 30 years old to serve for that year, or as much of it as they were needed. They were divided into ten 500-man juries called *decuries,* with the remaining dikasts on call as alternates. A really important case might call for the use of two or more decuries, so that as many as 2,500 men might be judging one case. The judges, also elected by lot, were not expected to know anything about the law and served only as sort of chairmen. There were no rules, there was no official whose job it was to know the law, and precedent was not followed. *Exegetai*, expounders of the law, might be present to advise the jury if asked, but the jury was not obliged to ask or to follow their advice. At the end of the trial the dikasts did not retire to discuss the evidence or testimony, but voted for their verdict then and there.

In Rome in the time of the Caesars a panel of 360 jurors listened to witnesses present the evidence in a murder trial, and then 81 of the 360 were chosen by lot to listen to the summations by the orators for each side. After the final speeches, which were restricted to a maximum of two hours for the prosecution and three hours for the defense (earlier they had been allowed to go on as long as they liked, but that proved unwise), each side could remove 15 jurors of its choice. The 51 remaining jurors then voted by secret ballot, with the majority winning.

Trial by jury, one of the great developments of English common law, was a by-product of the continuing disputes over land ownership during the first few centuries of Norman rule. William the Conqueror had rewarded his noble Normans, and assured their continued loyalty, by parceling out titles and land confiscated from the defeated Saxon lords. But exactly which bit had been parceled out to which baron and for how long (some were lifetime tenures that couldn't be inherited) took a long time to sort out—often by force of arms—and feudal tenure in twelfth-century Britain often resembled a bloody game of musical chairs.

The royal ministers developed a series of writs, or "assizes," to cover the various claims and define the type of trial to be used in each case. These assizes were sort of fill-in-the-blank forms to reduce each claim to as simple a series of questions as could be managed. There were four traditional ways of conducting lawsuits: **Trial by Oath**, in which the defendant swore a complicated oath—which he had to get exactly right—denying the charges, with a gallery of men ready to swear that they believed him. A good memory and a large enough gallery would insure victory. In **Proof by Witness** the litigants didn't take the oaths themselves, but brought in "compurgators," witnesses who swore under oath that they believed in the honesty of the claimant and the truth of his story. The winner was usually the one with the largest number of sworn witnesses. Only if each side had an equal number would the facts of the case be considered. In **Trial by Battle** the two parties, or their champions, met on the field of combat. God would, presumably, see that the right man won. (Although it had not been used for several hundred years, Trial by Battle was not officially eliminated in England until an act of Parliament in 1819.) **Trial by Ordeal** involved holding a red-hot iron or thrusting one's hand into boiling water, along with a similar faith in the justice of the almighty.

In 1166 or thereabouts, a writ known as the **Assize of Novel Disseizin** was devised. Under its rules, twelve good men and true who were neighbors of the claimants were called together to decide, based on their own knowledge and whatever additional information they might require, who truly owned the land. At first this new sort of trial was used only in property disputes, but its elegance and simplicity soon caused it to be used for a wide variety of civil suits. Within a short time it was also being used in criminal cases.

The advantages for the king and his ministers were great. A royal judge traveling circuit from faraway London would still supply the law, thus assuring a certain standardization of law all over the realm and a continued respect for the king's justice, and local men—with a knowledge of the country, of the people involved, and probably of the case itself—would judge the facts of the case, usually far better than an outsider could.

The number 12 for jury panels was considered to have divine overtones. As an early English legal explicator explained:

> *And first as to their number twelve: and this number is no less esteemed by our law than by Holy Writ. If the twelve apostles on their twelve thrones must try us in our eternal state, good reason has the law to appoint the number of twelve to try our temporal. The tribes of Israel were twelve, the patriarchs were twelve, and Solomon's officers were twelve. Therefore, not only matters of fact were to be tried by twelve, but of ancient times twelve judges were to try matters of law, in the Exchequer Chamber, and there are twelve counselors of state for matters of state; and he that wageth his law must have eleven others with him who believe he says true. And the law is so precise in this number of twelve, that if the trial be by more or less, it is a mistrial.*[4]

---

4. *From* Duncomb's Trials; *quoted in* The Prisoner at the Bar *by Arthur Train (Scribner's, 1926).*

The jury was seen as giving a protection to the rights of the common man against the rich and powerful. When Sir William Blackstone examined and compiled the common law in his *Commentaries on the Common Law* in 1765, the book immediately became a necessary part of the baggage of every lawyer in Britain and its American colonies. As to juries, Blackstone expounded that:

> . . . *a competent number of sensible and upright jurymen, chosen by lot from among those of middle rank, will be found the best investigators of truth, and the surest guardians of public justice. For the most powerful individuals in the state will be cautious of committing any flagrant invasion of another's right, when he knows that the fact of his oppression must be examined and decided by twelve indifferent men, not appointed until the hour of the trial; and that, when once the fact is ascertained, the law must of course redress it. This, therefore, preserves in the hands of the people that share which they ought to have in the administration of public justice, and prevents the encroachments of the more powerful and wealthy citizens.*

Recently an interesting inversion has happened in the logic of the jury trial. Now it is felt that a jury should possess knowledge neither of the case nor of the people involved before the trial, as it might prejudice their decisions. In Great Britain and Canada, laws have been passed forbidding the press to cover crimes in the sort of detail that would enable the reader to form an opinion about the perpetrator until after the trial. In the United States, which has no such law and probably under the First Amendment could not pass one, the heavy press coverage of some sensational cases has resulted in picking jurors who, in swearing that they know nothing of the defendant, the victim, or the crime, are either hermits, invincibly ignorant, or certainly lying.

SELECTING THE JURY

The immediate concern of the defense and prosecution on the first day of a trial is selecting the jury. Each side has a list of the talesmen (potential jurors), which they have carefully studied, and most of the people on the list have been investigated. The practice of jury selection varies greatly from state to state, but a typical practice might look like this: There are perhaps 120 names on the list, so the initial investigation is limited. Forty of these will be brought into the courtroom at a time, and twelve names will be selected at random from the 40 and seated in the jury box. This is the first batch of potential jurors, and they will now undergo the *voir dire* examination by the judge and the attorneys for the two sides.

Voir dire, which is French for "speak the truth," is the name given to the questioning of the jurors by the opposing attorneys—or, in some jurisdictions, by the judge on behalf of the attorneys—to determine whether they can be fair and unbiased. The prosecution and defense naturally have differing ideas on just what constitutes a fair and impartial juror. (Just to confuse things, "*voir dire* examination" is also the name given to a hearing held during the trial out of the jury's presence for the judge to determine whether a certain bit of evidence or testimony is admissible.)

The prosecution and defense are each allowed a specific number of "peremptory" challenges, by which they can remove prospective jurors from the panel with no reason given. This number varies from state to state, but 10 is about average. Prospective jurors are also excused "for cause," which occurs when there is some fact that has been disclosed that would make the prospective juror unfit to serve. This could include an inability to understand English well enough, or to follow directions, or an evident drinking or drug problem. It could also include a bias or prejudice against the defendant, the court system, law enforcement, the victim, doctors (if medical evidence is going to be important in the case), or a specific race or ethnic group of which someone involved is a member.

While conducting the *voir dire*, an attorney will zealously horde his stock of peremptory challenges, and will therefore try to find some "cause" to excuse a juror with whom he is unhappy.

Some of the *voir dire* examination questions are asked to determine any potential bias or prejudice:

- Do you know or have you ever had any business dealings with the defendant?
- Have you ever been arrested for a crime?
- Is anyone in your family a policeman or lawyer or court official?
- The defendant is an Etruscan. Have you had any business dealings with Etruscans? Are you related by marriage to an Etruscan?

- Have you heard any of the following popular sayings? How do you feel about them?

  "If you have an Etruscan for a friend you don't need any enemies."

  "The recipe for Etruscan chicken soup: first steal a chicken . . . "

  "The Etruscan national bird used to be a vulture, but they ate it."

  Do you know any other Etruscan stories or jokes? What are they? How do you feel about them?

Some might be asked in order to bring out facts that would enable the attorney to excuse the talesman "for cause," and often include facts established by an investigator checking the potential juror's background:

- Didn't you tell your fellow employees at the bratwurst factory that the police probably framed the case against the defendant, because you know for certain that they do that sort of thing all the time?
- Isn't it true that your wife's sister is married to the arresting officer?

Some might be asked to remind the jury of how they're supposed to behave:

- Do you believe you can be absolutely fair and impartial?
- Are you willing to follow the judge's instructions as to the law even if you disagree with them?
- Do you have any strong feelings about the death penalty, either way, that would make it difficult for you to judge the facts in this case?

In capital cases, prospective jurors are often subjected to searching questions about their attitudes toward the death penalty. A juror who would never vote to put a defendant to death can be excused for cause, as can one who would always vote for death for any defendant convicted of murder.

Sometimes attorneys go to extreme lengths in selecting jurors. The talesmen in the O.J. Simpson criminal trial had a 301-question questionnaire to fill out. (It is given in full in the Appendix at the back of this book.) Among the questions, proposed by one side or the other and agreed to by the judge, were:

8. Are you taking any form of medication?
17. Do you speak any language other than English?
22. Do you have the authority to hire and fire employees?
36. Do you plan to attend school in the future?
143. Have you ever asked a celebrity for an autograph?
284. Please name the three public figures you admire most.

Jury Consultants

The woman sitting at the defense table of the Lane case, Ms. Wanderlei, was a professional jury consultant, a job that has no specific training course but, rather, is re-created by each person who undertakes it. Depending on the consultant, the skills brought to the task vary from psychologist to statistician to psychic. Ms. Wanderlei had a list of all the talesmen along with all the information known about each one, and, as the juror selection process proceeded, she often would write little notes and pass them over to Artemus Porter. Hiring her had not been Porter's idea; he liked to be responsible for every aspect of the case himself, especially picking the jurors, but Broderick Lane had seen Wanderlei on a television show and been impressed by her. And, after all, it was his money and his life at stake.

The selection of the jury, including four alternates, took one month. This pleased the judge, as in capital cases it often takes much longer, sometimes more than three months. Judge Merkle then gave her admonition to the jury. "You are the sole judges of the facts in this case," she told them, "but I am the judge of the law. You will take your instructions from me. You will pay attention at all times and take no notes.[5]

"At the end of the trial you may request to have some specific bit of testimony read back to you if there is a problem, and I will probably allow it at that time. You will discuss the case with nobody, not even with each other, until it is given to you to consider at the end. If the defendant chooses not to testify, it is his constitutional right, and you are not to wonder about it or attribute any motive to it. If either counsel objects to any testimony and it is stricken, you are not to use it in your deliberations or speculate as to why it was stricken. These rules exist for the protection of the defendant and to insure the fairness of the judicial process, and I expect you to

---

5. *California and some other states now allow jurors to take notes.*

adhere to them. If you have any problems at any time, or if any of you need to pause for a rest-room break, or any other purpose, pass a note to the bailiff and he will give it to me."

The judge turned back to the courtroom and announced, "We will take a fifteen-minute recess, and then the prosecution may begin its opening statement."

•   •   •

The defense team in the O.J. Simpson murder trial used an experienced jury consultant named Jo-Ellan Dimitrius to assemble focus groups as stand-in juries. She asked them questions about how they would react if thus and so were true; how they would feel if this or that were discussed; what they thought of O.J. Simpson, of the Los Angeles Police Force, of black men who marry white women, and vice versa. Dimitrius found that, contrary to expectation, the group most likely to believe O.J. innocent, despite powerful evidence pointing to his guilt (one focus group was asked to assume that the glove was proven to be O.J.'s and that the blood splatters on the walk were also his), were black women, and further discovered that the less educated those women were, the more likely they were to affirm his innocence.

The assumption had been that women, and especially black women with a history of being mistreated by black men, would be sympathetic to Nicole. Instead, the focus groups showed that black women hated and resented her. As one writing team explained:

> They didn't criticize Simpson for living an upscale white lifestyle, leaving his community behind. That wasn't important. He'd left them long ago. The gut issue was Nicole. This white woman had lived their fantasy. She had things they should have. The team was stunned. The women came close to calling Nicole a whore. They came right to the edge of suggesting she got what she deserved. . . . virtually every middle-aged African-American woman in the focus group supported Simpson and resented the murder victim.[6]

Armed with that knowledge, the defense team went out of its way to assemble a jury composed—as much as possible—of black women.

---

6. *Lawrence Schiller and James Willwerth,* American Tragedy: The Uncensored Story of the Simpson Defense.

Since the number of peremptory challenges they were allowed was limited, they created a massive jury questionnaire (see appendix) hoping that at least one answer from among the 301 questions would give them ammunition to challenge any of the prospective jurors they wanted for cause, if the judge allowed them to do so. And, leaning backward to appear fair, he did. In a city that is only 11 percent African-American, the defense managed to empanel a jury that had eight black women.

The prosecution team, not possessing the information from these focus groups (a jury expert offered to help them, but was turned down), and believing that black women would make good jurors for the prosecution, was sandbagged.

RULES FOR THE JURORS IN THE O.J. SIMPSON TRIAL

First Approximation
Realizing that the O.J. Simpson case was provoking unusual interest, and that this would present problems for the jury, Judge Lance Ito, with suggestions from the attorneys on both sides, drew up the following document:

1 Date: 23 September 1994
   Department 103
2 HON. LANCE A. ITO, Judge
   D. ROBERTSON, Deputy Clerk
3

4   SUPERIOR COURT OF THE STATE OF CALIFORNIA

5   IN AND FOR THE COUNTY OF LOS ANGELES

6

7 PEOPLE   Case #BA097211

8   v   **COURT ORDER**

9 ORENTHAL JAMES SIMPSON

Each juror and alternate juror selected to serve in this matter is ordered and directed to:

1. Not to read or listen to or watch any accounts or discussions of this case reported by newspapers, television, radio, or any other news media.

2. Not to visit or view the premises or place where the offense or offenses charged were allegedly committed or any premises or place involved in this case unless directed by the court to do so.

3. Not to converse with other jurors or with anyone else upon any subject connected with the trial unless and until permitted to do so by the court.

4. Not to request, accept, agree to accept, or discuss with any person receiving or accepting, any payment or benefit in consideration for supplying any information concerning this trial for a period of 180 days from the return of a verdict or the termination of the case, whichever is earlier.

5. Promptly to report to the court any incident within their knowledge involving an attempt by any person improperly to influence any member of the jury.

Dated:_____, 19_____

_____
Hon. Lance A. Ito

I agree to the above order and understand that if I violate the provisions of this order that I can be ordered to pay a sanction to the court of up to $1,500 for each violation pursuant to Code of Civil Procedure Section 177.5, to reimburse or make payment to the County of Los Angeles for costs caused by a violation pursuant to California Rules of Court, Rule 227,

1 or punished by a fine or imprisonment for contempt pursuant to Code of

2 Civil Procedure Section 1218.

3   Dated:_____, 19_____

4

5   _____
                                                    Juror

Second Approximation

After about six weeks the attorneys and the judge decided that the first set of rules were not strong enough, so the following draconian regulations were devised:

1 Date: 12 December 1994
   Department 103
2 HON. LANCE A. ITO, Judge
   D. ROBERTSON, Deputy Clerk
3

4 SUPERIOR COURT OF THE STATE OF CALIFORNIA

5 IN AND FOR THE COUNTY OF LOS ANGELES

6

7 PEOPLE   Case #BA097211

8   v   **COURT ORDER**

9 ORENTHAL JAMES SIMPSON

10

11   During the course of this trial, and until further order of this court, the

12 trial jurors and alternates in this case shall NOT read any newspaper arti-

13 cle or other written account including magazines or books or watch any

14 television programs dealing with this case, the defendant or his family, the

15 victims or their families, the attorneys or any other matter concerning this

16 case. The court will distribute to the jurors and alternates the local daily

newspaper of their choice, edited to remove any coverage of this case.

Jurors and alternates shall <u>NOT</u> listen to any radio programming. Each juror and alternate may listen to audio tapes and compact disks, including books on tape that do not concern this case. Jurors and alternates who need current weather and traffic information may get this information by dialing (213) 962-3279.

Jurors and alternates shall <u>NOT</u> watch:

1. <u>ANY</u> television news program or news break.

2. <u>ANY</u> television "<u>tabloid</u>" program such as Hard Copy, A Current Affair, Inside Edition, American Journal, or Premiere Story.

3. <u>ANY</u> television <u>talk show</u> such as Marilu, Leeza, Jenny Jones, Sally Jessy Raphael, Oprah, Donahue, Good Morning America, Today, CBS This Morning, The Montel Williams Show, The Maury Povich Show, Ricki Lake, Rolonda, Rush Limbaugh and Geraldo.

4. <u>ANY</u> television news magazine program such as 60 Minutes, 20/20, Dateline, Eye to Eye, 48 Hours, or Primetime Live.

5. <u>ANY</u> entertainment news magazine such as Entertainment Tonight and EXTRA.

6. CNN, CNN Headline News, CNBC, The E! Channel, Sports Center on ESPN, Press Box on Prime Ticket, The News on MTV, any news or talk show on BET and Dennis Miller Live on HBO.

7. The Tonight Show (Jay Leno) and The Late Show with David Letterman.

1 | **Jurors and alternates MAY watch:**

2 | 1. Normal television entertainment programming, including sports and

3 | home shopping channels, not excluding above, however, jurors are strong-

4 | ly cautioned to avoid watching advertisements for upcoming news broad-

5 | casts known as "teasers."

6 | 2. Cable or satellite television channels: American Movie Classics,

7 | Showtime, Cinemax, The Disney Channel, The Movie Channel, The

8 | Shopping Channel, The Family Channel, The Cartoon Channel, Turner

9 | Classic Movies, MTV, Discovery Channel, Arts and Entertainment (A&E),

10 | Bravo, Lifetime, Nashville, Nickelodeon and Home Box Office.

11 | 3. Movies and other programming on video tape that do not involve

12 | this case, the defendant or his family, the victims or their families, or the

13 | attorneys and their families.

14 |

15 | Any questions regarding this order shall be directed to the Clerk of the

16 | Court.

17 |

18 | **IT IS SO ORDERED.**

SIX

THE PROSECUTION

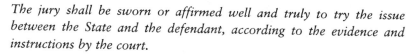

> *The jury shall be sworn or affirmed well and truly to try the issue between the State and the defendant, according to the evidence and instructions by the court.*
>
> — STATE OF WASHINGTON COURT RULES, 1993

On an episode of a television talk show called "Burden of Proof" that aired after the O.J. Simpson criminal trial was over, co-host Roger Cossack asked guest attorney Alan Dershowitz, who had worked on the Simpson defense team, "Alan, in your new book, *Reasonable Doubts,* you make the thesis that it really seems that it wasn't so much that the defense won this case as much as the prosecution lost it. . . . What does that say to people who aren't lawyers, about whether or not trials should be searches for truth?"

Dershowitz responded:

> [C]riminal trials are not searches for truth. You know, over 70 times in this case, both the prosecution and the defense claim they were searching for truth. Nonsense. If you wanted to have a search for truth, it would be very simple. You take the suspect in, you torture him, you torture his children, you'd search him. You would have no warrants. You would do everything that you could do, and you'd just go to China and Iran and Iraq to learn how to conduct a search for

99

truth. Or else you'd go to the scientific lab and you'd use the mecha-
nisms used in science. A criminal trial is not a whodunit and it's not
solely a search for truth. What it is, is an attempt to put the prosecution to its burden. And the prosecution's burden of proof is not simply to persuade the jury that the defendant did it, or even that he did
it beyond a reasonable doubt, but that by admissible, noncorrupt evidence, the standard of beyond a reasonable doubt has been met. And
that didn't happen in this case.

That might seem a bit cynical, even for a Harvard Law School professor, and one of its basic assertions doesn't seem to be true. Torture
produces what the torturer wants to hear; sometimes it is truth, often
it is not. Any "search for truth" can be objective only up to a point.
Neither torture nor scientific analysis can produce the truth with certainty. A "search for truth" conducted in any way but through an
adversarial trial may soon become a search for the answer that is
desired by those in authority. As Professor Dershowitz suggests, our
criminal trial system—flawed as it is—and the "burden of proof"
requirement for the prosecution are the best protectors of the innocent
yet devised.

OPENING STATEMENTS

Assistant District Attorney Carter Weiss had spent some time preparing his open-
ing statement. It was not flowery or verbose, but instead was direct and forceful. He
began by introducing himself and his associates to the jury, as though they hadn't
all seen enough of him over the past weeks while the panel was being selected. Then
he introduced the judge, the defendant and the defense team, and the court clerk.
He thanked the jury for the service they were about to perform and gave them a
short history of juries, showing them their place in the criminal justice system and
how important it was. The subtle effect of all this impartial information was to con-
vince the jury that he was a nice guy, and that he, as a representative of the State,
and thus the people—indeed the very people sitting in the jury box—was interested
only in justice. And then he settled down to tell them what justice would consist of in
this case.

"The State will prove beyond a reasonable doubt that Broderick Lane committed
a vicious double murder," he told the jury. "Now, you are going to hear the term

'beyond a reasonable doubt' many times during the course of this trial. Let me tell you what it means—and what it does not mean.

"It means that the State's story of the crime, supported by testimony and evidence, must convince you that it is the most plausible, most reasonable re-creation of the murders of Lucille Lane and J.J. Johansohn. That it fits the facts of the case and leaves no reasonable doubt that the defendant committed the crime. It does not mean no doubt whatever. It does not mean that our version must be the only possible scenario, and that there is, in the words of W.S. Gilbert, 'no manner of doubt; no probable, possible shadow of doubt; no possible doubt whatever.'

"A shadow of doubt can always be raised by a skillful defense attorney. Perhaps it was all an incredible coincidence; perhaps it was part of a deep-laid plot against the defendant by unseen and unknown enemies; perhaps aliens landed in flying saucers and committed the murders."

Weiss went over to the jury box and stared earnestly at the jurors. "Or perhaps," he said, his voice low and compelling, "as we will show by convincing evidence, Broderick Lane, in an act compounded of jealousy and a desire to save himself an expensive divorce, killed his wife and her lover in cold blood and with premeditation."

Weiss then told the jury who his principal witnesses would be and what he expected to show by their testimony. Then he sat down.

Artemus Porter stood up, surveyed the jury, then announced that, with the judge's permission, he would reserve his opening remarks, and sat back down.

The prosecution called its first witness.

THE WHOLE TRUTH

Thou shalt not bear false witness against thy neighbor...

—Exodus 20:16

All witnesses must take a sworn oath to tell the truth while on the witness stand, unless the act of swearing is repugnant to them because of their religious beliefs or meaningless to them because of their lack thereof, in which case they are allowed to "affirm." The oath, delivered by the judge, the court clerk, or a bailiff designated by the court, usually with the witness's right hand raised and left hand on the Bible, is some variant of the form: "I, [state your name], do solemnly swear that the evidence I shall give shall be the truth, the whole truth and nothing but the truth, so help me God." The "so help me God" is sometimes left off.

The British put God first: "I swear by Almighty God that the evidence. . . . "

The oath serves to impress the solemnity of the occasion upon the witness and to place upon him the strictures of both God and man to be truthful. Early Christians believed that to lie under oath was to break one of the major commandments and would result in their being immediately struck down by the Almighty. With the rise of feudalism, oath-breaking became a question of honor, and this was an age when people revered their honor above all else that was not directly in the provenance of their religion. Today the oath is backed up with the power of the court, and perjury is a criminal offense.

Although most courts supply a King James Bible to swear on, containing both Old and New Testaments, it should be recognized by those interested in minutia that Christians swear on the New Testament, while Jews swear on the Old. Moslems are sworn on their bible, which is the Koran. Some Baptists will not swear at all, but only affirm, because of their interpretation of the Gospel according to St. Matthew, Chapter 5, Verses 34 and 35: "But I say unto you, Swear not at all; neither by heaven; for it is God's throne; / Nor by the earth; for it is his footstool: neither by Jerusalem; for it is the city of the great King."

Those native Chinese who are not Christians have informed the courts of a variety of practices that would make an oath binding to them. One involves blowing out a candle, another sacrificing a white cockerel, and yet another breaking a saucer. Buddhists have been sworn with the following oath: "I declare, as in the presence of Buddha, that I am unprejudiced and if what I speak shall prove false, or if by coloring truth others shall be led astray, then may the Three Holy Existences, Buddha, Dharma, and Pro Sangha, in whose sight I now stand, together with the Devotees of the twenty-two Firmaments, punish me and also my migrating soul."

An oath is considered properly given if the court in which the witness takes it has the authority to administer it, and if it is so performed and phrased that the witness accepts it without question or states that he or she considers it binding. The Federal Rules of Evidence are flexible on the question of oaths, merely specifying that "[b]efore testifying, every witness shall be required to declare that the witness will testify truthfully, by oath or affirmation administered in a form calculated to awaken the witness' conscience and impress the witness' mind with the duty to do so" (Rule 603).

According to statute in California (Evidence Code section 710), when the witness is a child under 10, the judge, in her discretion, may dispense with the oath and substitute a promise from the child to tell the truth.

The criminal justice system not only differs in every state, but it is also—from place to place, at different speeds and in different ways—constantly changing. At the same time forces are pulling the various codes, customs, and statutes together, other forces are pushing them apart. Yet the face of the law, as seen by people in criminal courtrooms across the country, varies little from place to place. The order in which the elements of a criminal trial unfold is fixed by custom, if not by statute, and remains fairly constant from state to state and from decade to decade. After the jury is selected and sworn in, the prosecutor gives his opening statement, in which he outlines the elements of the crime and gives the jury the State's view of how, why, and by whom (the defendant, of course) the crime was committed. He may also brief the jury on what witnesses he expects to call and what each of them will contribute to the story of the crime that will be unfolding.

The defense attorney ordinarily gives her opening statement next, although in some courts she will be allowed to choose to give it after the State rests and before she presents her witnesses. In her opening statement she may present an alternate theory of the crime, which she will try to prove through her witnesses, or she may cast doubt on the logic of the State's case or the honesty and probity of the State's witnesses. If she is not planning to put the defendant on the stand, she may stress to the jury that the defendant has an absolute right not to testify, and that the jury is to make nothing of this.

The prosecuting attorney presents his case-in-chief first, in which he attempts to prove everything he asserted in his opening statement. The logic of this is inescapable: The defense has to hear the prosecution's case in order to know what to defend against. The prosecutor calls his witnesses to establish the facts that build his case. The defense attorney cross-examines these witnesses to try to tear holes in the prosecution's case or to establish a basis for her theory of the case, one in which the defendant is not guilty.

Then the prosecution, having told its story with the best available witnesses and physical evidence, rests its case-in-chief. If the prosecution's case seems weak, the defense counsel may at this time enter a motion to dismiss it. This is a motion for the judge to rule that the prosecution has not made a strong enough showing of facts for there to be anything for the jury to consider. If the defense really believes that the prosecution's case was fatally weak, and the motion to dismiss is denied, the defense can rest without presenting any witnesses. The defense, after all, doesn't have to prove anything.

●   ●   ●

Weiss first put a series of police and other technical witnesses on the stand. First up were the first officers, Abercrombie and Bull; then came detectives Desilva and Brown, who recounted the events of the morning the bodies were discovered. After first "refreshing their memories" from their notebooks, the first officers and the detectives described the crime scene as they saw it when they arrived: no visible signs of a robbery or attempted robbery, and the two victims lying there partially—mostly—undressed, dead of bullet wounds. Weiss put emphasis on the lack of visible signs of robbery.

In cross-examination, Porter had the officers admit that they were concerned with murder and were only superficially interested in the possibility of robbery. "No visible signs of a robbery" meant merely that nothing was disturbed to their eyes. The lack of anything pointing to a robbery in their memory-refreshing notebooks might only have been because they were not looking for such signs.

●   ●   ●

Ninety years ago, prosecutor Arthur Train commented on memory-refreshing as follows:

> The common doctrine of what is known as "refreshing the memory" in actual practice is notoriously absurd. Witnesses who have made memoranda as to certain facts, or even, in certain cases, of conversations, and who have no independent recollection thereof, are permitted to read them for the purpose of "refreshing" their memories. Having done so, they are then asked if they *now* have, *independently of the paper*, any recollection of them. In ninety-nine cases out of a hundred it would be absolutely impossible for them really to *remember* anything of the sort. They read the entry, know it is

probably accurate, and are morally convinced that the fact is as there-on stated. They answer *yes*, that their recollection *has* been refreshed and that they now do remember, and are allowed to testify to the fact as of their own knowledge.[1]

* * *

Next the prosecution called the deputy medical examiner who had looked at the bodies on the scene and the forensic technicians who had examined the scene for physical evidence. Weiss then attempted to introduce crime scene photographs into evidence so that he could show them to the jury to illustrate the detectives' descriptions.

Porter promptly objected, on the grounds that the photographs of the victims were overly gory and distressing, and would unduly inflame the jury.

Judge Merkle adjourned the trial and told the jurors to take a two-hour lunch so that she would have time to go over the pictures herself and decide which were proper and which were inflammatory.

* * *

When presented with physical evidence that is particularly gory or potentially upsetting or inflammatory to the jury, the judge has to weigh the probative value that the prosecution insists the evidence possesses against the prejudicial effect the defense is sure will result. Probative means "proving," and often what the prosecution wants to prove by crime-scene photographs in a murder trial is that the murder was particularly horrible and cruel, just what the defense would like to suppress. There have been many instances where the prosecution's case was not particularly strong, but the crime was so horrific that the jury needed to convict someone, and the defendant was the only one at hand.

OBJECTIONS

As noted trial attorney Melvin Belli has explained:

> Facts are presented to a jury by "evidence." That's a system of legal rules evolved from the common law. . . . It's been tried and tested.

---

1. *Arthur Train*, The Prisoner at the Bar. (Italics in the original.)

Evidence is an *exclusionary*, rather than an *affirmative*, science. That means it tells you more specifically what you can't prove and how you can't prove it, than what and how you can. . . . Objections to evidence are rarely based on newly conceived legal points. The right to so object has been time-tested. Time and again, in the past, the same point, the same objection, to the introduction of the same evidence, sustained or over-ruled, has achieved the fairest result for both sides.[2]

A trial attorney objects when he realizes that the opposition is about to introduce testimony or evidence that he feels the jury should not see or hear. The grounds for these objections are formalized, and the judge sustains or overrules them based on their legal validity. If the judge rules incorrectly on an objection, this can be one of the grounds for an appeal of the verdict. Many times, lawyers will make objections that they know are going to be overruled in order to get the objection in the record so it can be considered on appeal. In many states, if a lawyer does not enter a timely objection to questionable evidence or testimony and cite proper grounds for the objection, then that point cannot be brought up on appeal.

Whether to object to a given exchange or bit of evidence is often a delicate decision for the trial lawyer. Getting the objection on record for use in a possible appeal must be balanced against the possibility that jumping up and shouting, "I object!" may draw the jury's attention to a bit of problematic evidence that otherwise might just slide by unnoticed. And the decision as to whether to object, and on what grounds, must be made the instant the objectionable utterance comes from the examining attorney's mouth—surely not the least of the necessary talents of a good trial lawyer.

The trial judge has a different, but related, problem in responding to objections. It is one of the vexations of trial judges—who hate to have their cases overturned on appeal—that objections on which they are expected to rule with the speed of plate umpires calling a pitch can be examined, studied, parsed, dissected, and put into historical perspective by appellate court justices who can take all the time they need to review any aspect of the case they are examining.

---

2. *Melvin M. Belli,* "Ready for the Plaintiff!" (Italics in the original.)

Some of the objections one might expect to hear during the course of a criminal trial are:

"I object, your honor—"

"That is not the best evidence." This could come up, for example, if the examining attorney asks a detective, "What caliber of gun shot the fatal bullets?" If a firearms expert has examined the bullets and the detective planned to base his testimony on the work of the expert, then the testimony of the expert would be the best evidence, and the opposing attorney has a right to call for it.

"That is beyond the scope of the direct examination." This is an objection to a subject on which the witness is being cross-examined that does not relate to a matter brought up in the direct examination. Cross-examination is supposed to be limited to a scrutiny of the direct examination.

"No proper foundation has been laid." This is the opposing attorney's way of making sure evidence is presented in its appropriate order. If a gun is introduced into evidence, for example, an attempt must be made to show that it is the murder weapon or has some other relevance to the crime before it would be proper to trace its ownership.

"That calls for speculation on the part of the witness." This is stated in response to a question such as, "How many people do you think the bomb would have killed if it had gone off inside the cheese factory?" or "What did you think Ralph was going to do with the knife?" The witness is being asked for her opinion, and not for a fact. Such opinions would be regarded as beyond the scope of a lay witness. In most jurisdictions a witness is allowed to express an opinion on matters of common experience. If asked "What was Ralph's mental attitude when he left the building?" the response "He seemed to be angry" would probably be acceptable. Most of us know what anger looks like. "He acted as if he had gone crazy" would likewise probably pass. "He was a schizophrenic in the grips of a severe delusional episode" would be challenged unless the witness was a mental health professional.

The only witnesses allowed to express opinions on specialized subjects are expert witnesses, whose opinions are putatively backed by great learning, and even they are allowed to express opinions only on the subject of their expertise.

"That is hearsay." This is used in response to the witness saying something like, "Jack and Jill told me they went up the hill to fetch a pail of water." If the examining attorney wants to bring out what Jack and Jill said, he should question Jack and Jill. Hearsay testimony is excluded because it is not the best evidence, and also because it gives the opposing attorney no chance to cross-examine the person(s) supposedly making the statement.

"That's been asked and answered." This is used to prevent the examining attorney from worrying the witness like a dog worrying a bone, and going after the same point from as many different directions as possible.

"Incompetent, irrelevant, and immaterial." This objection, each part of which may be made separately, is a sort of catch-all way of saying that the testimony called for is not relevant to the case.

"Three fifty-two, Your Honor." In California, 352 is the article in the Evidence Code that covers several grounds for objection. It reads:

> The court in its discretion may exclude evidence if its probative value is substantially outweighed by the probability that its admission will (a) necessitate undue consumption of time or (b) create substantial danger of undue prejudice, of confusing the issues, or of misleading the jury.

Defense attorney Porter's objection to the gory photographs would be a 352 objection, as it might (b) create substantial danger of undue prejudice (Federal Rules of Evidence 403 is the Federal court system's equivalent rule).

In making an objection, the attorney has to consider its effect on the jury. If the jurors feel that they are being prevented from hearing something that they would have found interesting, or that the attorney is merely being obstructive, then no amount of judicial admonition can prevent them from feeling hostile to the attorney, and thus less well disposed to his client.

Contrary to the established wisdom of jury selection, William Joseph Fallon, a great trial lawyer of the early part of the twentieth century, was known for taking the first jurors offered. He explained his philosophy thus: "When I accept a jury right off, it makes them think

I am some pumpkins. They are psychologically for me. Later on, when I do object to something, they think I have a solid, worth-while reason."[3]

•   •   •

When the court reconvened after the long lunch break, attorney Weiss had the permissible pictures of the crime scene passed among the jurors. Judge Merkle had disallowed the particularly gory close-ups of the bodies, but those she had allowed effectively made the prosecution's point.

Weiss's next witness was Daniel Petrov, the jewelry store employee who had found Johansohn's body. After a few questions that identified the witness to the jury, Weiss asked him to describe finding the body:

> **Petrov:** *I just walked into the office and there he was. Mr. Johansohn, I mean. Lying there. And all that blood. I looked around the office to see, you know, what had happened, if anything had been disturbed or whatever, and then I went to the telephone on the sales floor and called the police.*
>
> **Weiss:** *If there had been anything out of the ordinary, I mean besides the dead body, you would have seen it.*
>
> **Petrov:** *Yes, certainly.*
>
> **Weiss:** *If anything was disturbed or out of place, I mean, if, say, someone had attempted to burglarize the store, you would have noticed.*
>
> **Petrov:** *Of course. There was no sign that the store had been robbed.*
>
> **Weiss:** *Or that a robbery had been attempted?*
>
> **Petrov:** *No, not that, either. I would have seen.*

By this testimony, Weiss was attempting to close one of the holes through which Broderick Lane could wiggle: the possibility that the murders had happened during the course of an attempted burglary or robbery. It was now Artemus Porter's job to reopen, and if possible enlarge, the hole. He got up to cross-examine.

CROSS-EXAMINATION

In his book *My Life in Court*, esteemed attorney Louis Nizer discusses cross-examination:

---

3. *Gene Fowler,* The Great Mouthpiece.

Cross-examination is the only scalpel that can enter the hidden recesses of a man's mind and root out a fraudulent resolve. Psychiatry and drugs may have given us new insights into motivation, but the classic Anglo-Saxon method of cross-examination is still the best means of coping with deception, of dragging the truth out of a reluctant witness, and assuring the triumph of justice over venality.

The ability to conduct an effective cross-examination is one of the most important skills in the arsenal of the trial attorney, as well as one of the most difficult to master. If the witness, as is usually the case, is telling the truth as he knows it, but that truth is overly slanted in the favor of, say, the prosecution, then the defense attorney must bring that truth back toward or past the middle by careful questioning. However, if she is too assertive with a likable witness who appears to be honestly trying to tell the truth, then she runs the risk of alienating the jury and undoing any good she accomplishes in the examination.

One question on cross-examination that tends to be productive is, "Have you discussed your testimony with the state's attorney or anyone from his office?" The answer almost has to be "yes," because the prosecutor would be foolish to put anyone on the stand without knowing what he or she is going to say. But many witnesses think that it's wrong to admit to having talked about their testimony. Consequently, they will often hem and haw and deny it, and end up looking furtive when they are forced to admit that, yes, they spoke to the prosecutor twice in his office.

It is the lying witness that presents the cross-examiner's greatest challenge. Witnesses lie for many reasons. Some are trying to shield themselves or their kin, some wish to harm the defendant, and some are merely trying to bolster their own importance. People have been known to testify to seeing a crime they didn't see merely to have something to brag about to their friends, possibly thinking, "What the hell, the defendant's probably guilty anyway." A frontal assault on the witness's story will seldom accomplish more than to entrench him in his lie, but the astute cross-examiner, like the experienced military commander, will find some weak point to attack and then close all possible holes before attacking. Even the most trivial part of a lying tale will serve to discredit the whole if the witness can be induced to swear to its truth with sufficient fervor before it is exposed as a lie.

● ● ●

Something in Petrov's testimony rang a faint bell, the little bell of contradiction that sounds in the mind of a good trial attorney when a witness says anything that doesn't completely agree with prior statements. So, after a few preliminary questions:

Porter: *Let's see—you said that you didn't see any signs of a break-in or burglary, is that right?*

Petrov: *That's so.*

Porter: *And you would have?*

Petrov: *Of course. I—*

Porter: *You're very observant?*

Petrov: *I like to think so.*

Porter: *Nothing gets by you, is that right?*

Petrov: *Well . . .*

Porter: *Certainly nothing as big as a burglary or robbery?*

Petrov: *Of course not.*

Porter: *[to the judge] May I approach the witness? [to the witness] Would you look at this, please? Here—where I have it marked.*

Weiss: *May I see that?*

Porter: *It's a transcript of the 911 call made that morning. I believe you have a copy.*

Weiss: *Oh.*

Porter: *[to witness] Do you remember this call? Are these your words?*

Petrov: *I'll take your word for it. I was rather excited.*

Porter: *Do you have any doubts that these are your words? I can get the tape.*

Petrov: *No, no. This appears to be what I said.*

Porter: *Would you read there, where I have it marked? Read it aloud, if you don't mind.*

Petrov: [reading] *"It's my boss, Mr. Johansohn. He's dead. Murdered. In his office. I just opened the store and found him there."*

"[911 operator] Is anyone else there?"

"[caller] No. I don't think so. No."

"[911 operator] Okay. I've dispatched a police car. They'll arrive in a minute. Please just stay where you are."

Porter: *That will do, thank you. Now, I notice that you didn't tell the operator about Lucille Lane, whose body was lying in plain sight. Didn't you see her?*

Petrov: *I was preoccupied.*

Porter: *Did you see her body?*

Petrov: *I didn't think it necessary—*

Porter: *You didn't see her, did you? You didn't tell the first officers about her, you didn't tell the detectives about her. I can bring them back to the stand and ask them. You didn't see her, did you?*

Weiss: [to the judge] *Your honor, he's badgering the witness.*

Judge: *This is a cross-examination. I don't think it's out of line yet. I'll allow it.*

Porter: *You didn't see her, did you?*

Petrov: *She was in the other room.*

Porter: *You didn't see her, did you?*

Petrov: *No, I didn't.*

Porter: *So when you say you didn't see anything out of the ordinary, you missed something the size of a human body.*

Petrov: *I guess so, if you want to put it that way.*

Porter: *Let's see what else you might have missed. Isn't it true that Mr. Johansohn often had large amounts of cash on his person?*

Petrov: *Yes, I believe so.*

Porter: *Many thousands of dollars?*

Petrov: *Yes.*

Porter: *For the purpose of buying jewelry?*

Petrov: *Yes.*

Porter: *And that sometimes these transactions were done late at night in Mr. Johansohn's office?*

Petrov: *Yes.*

Porter: *Isn't that a bit irregular?*

Petrov: *It was not my place to question Mr. Johansohn.*

Porter: *Why do you think Mr. Johansohn conducted these midnight transactions?*

Weiss: [to the judge] *I object—calls for speculation on the part of the witness.*

Judge: *Sustained.*

Porter: *Do you know, of your own knowledge, why your boss carried these large sums of cash about?*

Petrov: *There are people who don't want to be seen selling their jewelry.*

Porter: *What sort of people?*

Petrov: *Well, wives who don't want their husbands to know; mistresses who don't want their boyfriends to know; men who are selling their wives' or mistresses' jewelry and replacing them with paste duplicates. That sort of thing.*

Porter: *Did Johansohn ever purchase stolen jewelry?*

Petrov: *If so, I am not aware of it.*

Porter: *Of course not, but he may have?*

Petrov: *I suppose so.*

Porter: *And that would also have been at night?*

Petrov: *I suppose so.*

• • •

It is in cross-examination that the defense attorney must plant the seeds for the alternate version of the crime that she hopes the jury will accept. In this case, defense attorney Porter was using a prosecution witness to suggest that J.J. Johansohn may have been carrying a large amount of money on him, and that some of his clients may have been less than honest. He would bolster and extend this theory with his own witnesses.

The witness was not deliberately lying, but was just following the suggestions of the prosecuting attorney. If you ask the average man whether he is observant, he will not deny it. Then, if subtly and gradually pushed, he can often be induced into believing that he saw more than he actually did, or saw things other than as they were.

At the turn of the century, Judge Edward Abbot Perry observed that:

> . . . while the testimony given by the average citizens in the courts is singularly free from the taint of perjury, yet if, on the other hand, you were to ask me whether, after a third of a century's experience of listening to sworn testimony in our courts, I was deeply impressed by the accuracy, reliability and truth of the daily round of evidence it has been my duty to consider, I should with sincere regret be bound to admit that the answer was in the negative. . . . I am glad to know myself, and I hope I have convinced my fellow citizens that most of the errors of testimony are due to defective observations, false reminiscences, the deflecting influence of suggestion and the pleasure of imagination.[4]

Cross-examination is a delicate instrument that, in the hands of a skilled trial attorney, can demolish testimony and change the course of a trial. But in the hands of a less-than-skilled practitioner, it can backfire.

My attorney friend Jack told me of a probably apocryphal story that had been told to him when he was trying his first court case. While cross-examining a witness he inadvertently brought out information that was harmful to his client. As he sat down, an older, wiser attorney leaned forward and whispered, "Don't feel bad. I, too, once asked one question too many."

Over lunch the old attorney explained: "When I was just starting out I was defending a man accused of biting another man's ear off in a dispute on a subway platform—the West Fourth Street stop of the Eighth Avenue Line, Uptown side. I asked a witness, 'Did you actually see my client bite that man's ear off?'

---

4. *Judge Edward Abbot Perry,* What the Judge Thought.

"'No,' the witness admitted.

"That's when I asked the one question too many. 'Then how do you know he did?!' I demanded.

"'Cause I seen him spit it out!'"

"When you get yourself in a mess like that, there's no way to save yourself verbally, no follow-up question to ask that won't just make things worse," Jack said. "The best thing to do is shut up and sit down. That's when I learned the Law of Holes."

"The Law of Holes?" I asked.

"When you're in one, stop digging."

LINCOLN ON CROSS

During the 23 years that Abraham Lincoln practiced law there were no court stenographers; hence no verbatim records exist of his courtroom technique. However, it is clear that his reputation as an outstanding trial lawyer was well deserved. The story of one of his later cases has become a legal legend and an exemplar of the art of cross-examination.

The defendant, Lincoln's client, was a lad named William "Duff" Armstrong, the son of an old friend of Lincoln's who had died a few years before. When Lincoln heard of William's trouble he wrote to Hannah Armstrong, the boy's mother, volunteering to take the case without a fee.

Armstrong was charged with the murder of James Preston Metzker, which resulted from a fight on Saturday, August 29, 1857. There was an eyewitness to the killing, and popular sentiment in Mason County, Illinois—where the crime was committed—was strongly against Armstrong.

Lincoln obtained a change of venue to Beardstown, Illinois, where the trial was held on Saturday, May 8, 1858. Lincoln appeared completely relaxed and almost uninterested while the prosecutors, Hugh Fullerton and J. Henry Shaw, made their case. It wasn't until after the eyewitness, a young man named Charles Allen, had testified that Lincoln seemed to take an interest. Allen told the court that he was a witness to the altercation, which had taken place at about eleven o'clock that Saturday night; that he had been about 150 feet away; and that he had seen Armstrong strike the fatal blow. Lincoln rose to cross-examine:

"How did you manage to see clearly at that time of night?" Lincoln asked.

"By the moonlight."

"And was there enough light to see everything that happened?"

Allen swore that there was, that the moon had been almost full.

Lincoln took an 1857 almanac from the table and had it entered into evidence. Then he handed it to Allen and asked him to read the entry for Saturday, August 29, 1857. The almanac revealed that the moon was nowhere near full, and had set shortly after eleven, so that it was so low on the horizon at the time of the killing as to provide almost no light.

The almanac branded Allen a liar, and the jury acquitted Armstrong on the first ballot.

It may be worth noting, in view of the insistence of many lawyers today that it is their ethical duty to defend a client no matter how heinous they may personally believe his actions to have been, that Lincoln did not share this view. An early Lincoln biographer, Frederick Trevor Hill, tells that one time when Lincoln discovered that a client was guilty of fraud he walked out of the courtroom and refused to continue the case. The judge sent a messenger asking him to return. "Tell the judge that my hands are dirty," Lincoln told the emissary, "and I have gone away to wash them."

● ● ●

On redirect examination of Mr. Petrov, the prosecution asked:

Q: *Isn't there a safe in the office?*
A: *Yes, there is.*

Q: *Wouldn't Mr. Johansohn keep any large sums of money in the safe?*
A: *Certainly.*

On re-cross, Porter asked:

Q: *Was there any money found in the safe when it was opened?*
A: *No.*

Q: *Haven't you seen Mr. Johansohn walking around with large sums of money on his person?*
A: *Yes.*

Q: *Even though there was a safe right there in the office?*
A: *Yes.*

The give-and-take between the prosecution and the defense continued through the rest of the prosecution's case.

A DNA expert testified to finding blood matching Lucille Lane's on Broderick Lane's shoes. Porter established that there was no way to tell when the blood was spilled on the shoes.

A criminalist testified to giving Lane a gunshot residue test the day after the murders and finding indications on his palms that he had fired a gun recently. On cross-examination, he admitted that he couldn't tell what gun was fired or when the gun was fired, and that it could have been any gun fired any time over a period of 48 hours or more.

Firearms expert Darrell Langert testified that he had examined the bullets removed from the bodies and that they were .28-caliber slugs fired from a Fosdick-Hubbart, a very rare gun. Even the bullets were almost impossible to obtain. He explained how he could tell, showing blow-up pictures of the marks on the slugs and explaining how they were made by the lands and grooves of the barrel. Langert further testified that he had discovered that a Fosdick-Hubbart was registered to Broderick Lane, but that, when questioned, Lane was unable to produce it and claimed not to know what happened to it.

In a further bombshell, Langert testified that he had removed some slugs from the basement shooting range at the Lane mansion and found some of them to be from a Fosdick-Hubbart. When viewed under the comparison microscope they were "not inconsistent with the slugs removed from the two bodies."

Porter's cross-examination was brief; he didn't want the firearms expert's testimony to linger on the jury's minds. He made the point that "consistent with" was not the same as a positive identification, and that the slugs were too mashed for a positive identification. Then he sat down.

Witnesses testified to having seen Broderick Lane yell at or slap Lucille Lane on more than one occasion. The defense cross-examination tried to show that these were no more than love spats.

Witnesses testified to having seen J.J. Johansohn and Lucille Lane together at various places around town for half a year before the murder. Defense attorney Porter asked one of them if he knew any other people who were cheating on their spouse. He said, "Yes." "And how many of them have been murdered?" Porter asked.

Jack Foxx, the operative from the firm of private detectives that Lane had hired, testified that he had followed Lucille Lane to her trysts and reported back to Broderick Lane. Porter elicited from Foxx that Lane had said that he wanted the information for his own protection in case Lucille Lane started divorce proceedings, and that Lane had never made any threats against his wife in Foxx's hearing.

Oliver Hamlet, a homeless man who slept in an alcove in the alley behind the jewelry store, testified that he had seen a black Mercedes pull up to the rear door the *night of the murder and a man who looked remarkably like Broderick Lane get out. The man entered the store for a short time—"maybe ten minutes," Hamlet judged— and then left and drove away. He had heard sounds that might have been gunshots, but he couldn't tell from what direction they came.*

On cross-examination it was brought out that he was homeless because he had a drinking problem. But Hamlet insisted that he was not drunk that night. He stuck to his story, but was made to sound vague and unsure of himself.

And so, having woven a strong web of circumstantial evidence around the accused, the prosecution rested.

SEVEN

THE DEFENSE

> *Once I decide to take a case, I have only one agenda: I want to win. I will try, by every fair and legal means, to get my client off—without regard to the consequences.*
>
> — ALAN DERSHOWITZ
> *The Best Defense*

In many criminal trials the most important and difficult part of the defending attorney's job comes during the first half of the trial, when the prosecution is presenting its evidence. Discrediting the prosecution's case is at least as important as presenting the defense's own story.

The guilty defendant often has an advantage over the truly innocent defendant: he knows what actually happened. If he is clever, he can carefully tailor his defense to fit the recoverable facts. The secret advantage for the side of truth and justice is that so many criminals who think they're clever are mistaken. The innocent defendant, on the other hand, usually doesn't know what really happened and is at a loss to explain away the evidence connecting him to the crime.

THE EYEWITNESS

The most frightening sort of evidence for an innocent defendant to face is the honest but mistaken eyewitness.

—In 1984, Edward Honaker was convicted of rape and sent to a Virginia prison on the eyewitness testimony of the victim. He was released ten years later, after newly available DNA tests proved he could not have committed the crime.

—James Newsome was put in an Illinois prison in 1981 for the murder of a grocery store owner, with his conviction based on the testimony of three eyewitnesses. In 1994, fingerprint evidence developed from a new computer technique implicated another man and Newsome was released.

—In 1996, Walter Smith was released from an Ohio penitentiary after 10 years when newly available DNA testing proved that the two women he was convicted of raping had been mistaken in identifying him as their assailant.

There have been at least 60 similar cases in the past decade. We can but conjecture how many people remain in prison, convicted by honest but mistaken eyewitness testimony.

WITH MY OWN EYES

The most convincing testimony any trial lawyer could ask for is that of the eyewitness. What could be more dramatic then the pointing of an accusing finger from the witness stand and a firm voice declaiming, "It was him—I saw him do it!"

There is a classic experiment, repeated with endless variations in freshman psychology classrooms year after year, that is conducted something like this:

In the middle of the professor's lecture, the rear door is flung open and a young woman wearing a red dress and sneakers and carrying an umbrella runs in shouting, "They got applesauce over all the terminals—it's not my fault!"

A young man runs in behind her wearing jeans, cowboy boots, and a short black raincoat, and waving a banana. He shouts, "You've ruined everything! Now they'll never let me jump off the bell tower!"

They grapple in front of the class, and the woman takes the banana from the man and stabs him with it. A third person—who was evidently sitting in one of the front seats—suddenly rises, grabs the woman's umbrella, and hits her over the head with it. She falls down, and the other two carry her out by a side door.

The professor then asks everyone in the class to write a description of what just happened. Rarely does anyone in the class get all of the important details right. The banana will become a gun, a knife, a newspaper, or a spatula. The umbrella might become a cane, a crutch, or a football, or it may disappear entirely. The man might become a woman, the woman a man, and the third person might be unobserved or might split in twain. And the aural memory of the event is, if anything, even worse than the visual memory.

Two historical cases powerfully demonstrate the unreliability of eyewitness testimony: The misidentification of Joseph Parker in 1805 and the imprisonment of Adolf Beck for someone else's crime in 1895.

Joseph Parker was walking down a New York City street one day in 1805 when a strange woman accosted him and accused him of being her missing brother-in-law, one Thomas Hoag, who had disappeared two years before. He was put on trial for deserting his (Thomas Hoag's) family and was identified as Hoag by Hoag's wife, landlord, and employer. His own wife—of eight years—testified that he couldn't be Hoag. To settle the question, a close friend of Hoag's remembered that Hoag had a large knife-scar on the bottom of his foot. Parker removed his boot. He had no scar. Hoag, as far as I know, was never found.

Adolf Beck was walking down Victoria Street in London in 1895, when a woman of easy virtue, as they were described in those days, accused him of being "Lord Winton de Willoughby," who had defrauded her by writing a bad check. Taken to the police station, he was similarly identified by several other women whom "Lord Willoughby" had cheated. Two policemen compounded his troubles by identifying him as a "John Smith" who had been sent to prison for similar behavior some years earlier.

Beck was convicted and sentenced to seven years as a "recidivist," as repeat offenders were called. His attorney managed to have the recidivist charge stricken, as an inspection of the prison records showed that the original "John Smith" had been circumcised, while Beck was not. But Beck was not granted a new trial, even though evidence of "his" earlier conviction must have weighed heavily with the jury.

Three years after he was released from prison, Beck was arrested again for offenses similar to the first batch. He was again convicted on eyewitness identification, and this time he clearly was a recidivist, so he received a stiff sentence. Just before Beck was to be shipped off to prison, a man calling himself Thomas was arrested on similar charges. When the eyewitnesses were confronted with both Beck and Thomas, they realized that they had made a mistake. The eyewitnesses from his earlier trial were called in, and they also admitted that they had mistaken Beck for Thomas. Beck was released.

It is a common belief in our culture that memory is permanent and immutable, that somewhere in all of our minds, if only we could dredge it out, is a recollection of every last thing that ever happened to us, and that this memory is unchanging and accurate. However, evidence has been accumulating over the past half-century that memory is not complete, not accurate, and not unchangeable.

Dr. Elizabeth Loftus, a psychologist who has made the workings of memory her special study, believes that eyewitness testimony is too often mistaken—honestly mistaken, but mistaken nonetheless. In her book *Witness for the Defense*, she describes some of the psychological processes at work that can make a firmly held and honestly believed identification by an eyewitness absolutely mistaken:

> *Memories don't just fade, as the old saying would have us believe; they also grow. What fades is the initial perception, the actual experience of the events. But every time we recall an event, we must reconstruct the memory, and with each recollection the memory may be changed—colored by succeeding events, other people's recollections or suggestions, increased understanding or a new context.*

This processing of memory is constant and ongoing and, Dr. Loftus suggests, has "[e]normous powers—powers even to make us believe in something that never happened." And when an eyewitness, relying on an honestly believed but faulty memory, gives mistaken testimony, the damage can seldom be undone.

One final quote from Dr. Loftus:

> *Innocence comes into the courtroom, but it is not surrounded by a halo and a white cloud. It comes in disguised as guilt, looking like guilt, smelling like guilt; and when the eyewitness points at the defense table and says, "He did it! He's the one!" you can almost hear the nails being pounded into the coffin.*

• • •

Artemus Porter's job seemed very simple: he didn't have to prove that Broderick Lane was innocent, he didn't have to prove what really happened, he didn't have to be Perry Mason. He merely had to introduce into the minds of the jury a reasonable doubt.

The basis of American criminal law is that a defendant is presumed innocent until proven guilty "beyond a reasonable doubt." But what jurors will consider "reasonable doubt" varies from jury to jury, and occasionally from moment to moment. The presumptions of most jurors are not the presumptions of the law. Unless experience has given them a reason to think otherwise, jurors tend to think, with the rest of us, that the defendant must be guilty, or else why would he be on trial? It is this hidden presumption that defense attorneys must topple.

In his opening statement, which he had reserved until this point in the trial, Porter pounded on the fact that the prosecution's entire case was based on circumstantial evidence, and that each of the circumstances could have a perfectly innocent explanation besides the one the prosecution had suggested, one of which he would demonstrate as the case continued. He mouthed the words "circumstantial evidence" as a continuing refrain, managing to sound with each repetition as though the concept was beneath contempt, something to which no decent human being would stoop.

He began his presentation of witnesses with character witnesses, friends and business associates of Broderick Lane. They testified that Lane was the mildest of men, that he never lost his temper, that he never had anything to say about Lucille that wasn't sweet and kind. The prosecutor was not able to change their stories much on cross-examination, which was good. But Porter knew that such testimony was of only limited value, that juries instinctively know that, as Shakespeare put it, a man can "smile and smile, and be a villain."

THE EXPERT WITNESS

Porter prepared to face one of the strong points of the prosecution's case, the firearms evidence, by bringing on a firearms expert of his own.

Moishe O'Sullivan first qualified himself: after graduating from the University of Arkham with a degree in Pharmacology, he had gone to work for the Metropolis Police Department as a junior criminologist before taking a job with the FBI.

Q: *And what did you do with the FBI?*
A: *I was trained in general criminalistics, with emphasis on firearms. Over the years at the Bureau I came to specialize in all aspects of firearms.*

Q: *And then?*
A: *I retired from the FBI six years ago, and began my own consulting firm, the O'Sullivan Forensics Bureau.*

Q: *And what sort of clients employ your firm?*
A: *We have done work for police forces around the country as well as prosecutors, public defenders, and private trial attorneys such as yourself.*

Thus, Porter hoped, he established the impartiality of this witness, who worked for both the prosecution and the defense. Then, after getting O'Sullivan to cite his various degrees, awards, citations, and memberships in professional organizations, he got down to business:

Q: *Did you look over the firearms evidence in this case?*
A: *Yes, I did. At your request I went to the Metropolis Police Crime Lab and did my own study of the bullets recovered from the victim's bodies, as well as those found in the wall of Mr. Lane's range. Let me say that the people at the Metropolis Crime Lab were very helpful.*

Q: *And what did you find in relation to this evidence?*
A: *The spent bullets from the victims and those taken from the wall were of .28 caliber, and had been fired from a Fosdick-Hubbart revolver, one of the few weapons to use this caliber. The barrel markings made that clear. But in my opinion, it is impossible to tell for sure whether the same weapon fired the two sets of bullets.*

Q: *We have testimony that the Fosdick-Hubbart is not a common revolver.*
A: *That is so.*

Q: *What does that mean? How many of them are there?*
A: *Well, I checked the records. There are twelve hundred registered in the state of Arkham. And there are probably a few hundred more unregistered.*

Q: *And any of these could have fired the fatal bullets?*
A: *In my opinion, yes.*

Q: *So "uncommon" is a relative term?*
A: *Yes.*

Then the prosecution cross-examined:

Q: *Mr. O'Sullivan, you say it's impossible to tell for sure whether all the examined bullets were fired from the same gun.*
A: *That's right.*

Q: *What would you say the probabilities were?*
A: *I don't like to deal in probabilities.*

Q: *Yes, but as we know, very little in this life is absolutely certain. Let's figure the percentages. Would you say it's fifty percent probable that they were fired from the same weapon?*
A: *You could say that.*

Q: *Seventy-five percent?*
[pause]
A: *Well, yes.*

Q: *Eighty percent? I'm asking for your honest professional judgment.*
A: *Well, I might go as high as eighty percent, but I wouldn't go much above that.*

Q: *So it's somewhere between eighty and a hundred percent sure that all these bullets were fired from the same weapon?*
A: *Yes.*

Q: *Is there anything about the forensic examination that would indicate that the bullets were not fired from the missing gun? Anything at all?*
A: *No.*

Q: *That is all. Thank you, Mr. O'Sullivan.*

•　•　•

Expert witnesses are called to give testimony explaining or amplifying other evidence. They draw upon specialized knowledge and (usually) years of training in their craft or profession to make known to the jury the meaning of some fact in evidence, or at least the most reasonable inference that can be drawn from it. From within the criminalistics community come such experts as forensic pathologists, crime scene technicians, fingerprint analysts, blood splatter specialists, hair and fiber analysts, firearms experts, and forensic DNA analysts. It was hair and fiber evidence that probably secured the conviction of Wayne Williams for the murders of over a dozen children in Atlanta.

But often the expertise must be drawn from the general community. Psychologists and psychiatrists are often called to testify, or accountants might be called to explain some abstruse bookkeeping. At the trial of Bruno Hauptmann for kidnapping the Lindbergh baby, an expert on wood was called in to demonstrate how wood in a ladder found at the crime scene matched wood found in Hauptmann's attic. At the trial of O.J. Simpson for the murder of his wife and her friend, a glove expert was called in to discuss a pair of gloves associated with the crime scene. Serial killer Ted Bundy was convicted of murder partly on the testimony of a dentist who said that the teeth marks found on a victim were made by Bundy.

EXPERT WITNESSES PAST

In 1899, Roland Molineux was charged with the murder of Katharine Adams. He had supposedly been trying to kill her nephew, Harry Cornish, by anonymously mailing him some stomach medicine doctored with cyanide. Cornish passed it on to his aunt, who died after drinking it.

Over a dozen expert witnesses spoke for the prosecution, all testifying that the handwriting on the package was that of Molineux. He was convicted and sentenced to death. However, the sentence was overturned by the appellate court, and his case was sent back for retrial. A new, more stringent set of rules regarding, among other things, expert witnesses had come into force in the meantime, and much of the testimony from the first trial was not allowed at the second. This time Molineux was found innocent.

The criterion that judges used for many years in deciding whether scientific evidence was admissible in court was known as the Frye Test. It was formulated by the United States Court of Appeals for the District of Columbia in 1923, during the case of *Frye v The United States*, when the court was considering the admissibility of a polygraph (lie detector) test into evidence. The court decided that the major consideration was whether the new scientific technique was generally accepted by experts in that field. It said:

Just when a scientific principle or discovery crosses the line between the experimental and demonstrable stages is difficult to define. Somewhere in this twilight zone the evidential force of the principle must be recognized, and while courts will go a long way in admitting expert testimony deduced from a well-recognized scientific principle or discovery, the thing from which the deduction is made must be sufficiently established to have gained general acceptance in the particular field in which it belongs.

Since the Frye decision came down, it has been modified and broadened in both directions. The New York Court of Appeals has ruled (in *People v Middleton*, 1981) that the acceptance of the technique by experts need not be unanimous. Instead, the test should be "not whether a particular procedure is unanimously endorsed by the scientific community, but whether it is generally accepted as reliable." The Second Circuit Court of Appeals, weighing the admissibility of sound voice spectrometry or "voiceprint" evidence (in *The United States v Williams*), said that it was not sufficient for the scientific community to be satisfied as to the utility of a test, but that the court must also be satisfied. It is the job of the court to weigh the test's "probativeness, materiality, and reliability [against] . . . any tendency to mislead, prejudice or confuse the jury."

In the 1993 decision, *Daubert v Merrell-Dow*, the United States Supreme Court substituted for the Frye Rule a more complex test for admitting scientific evidence, which lower federal courts and the courts of those states that use the Federal Rules of Evidence are still trying to interpret.

Other states have gone their own way. The Supreme Court of the State of California ruled in 1994 that, at least in California, the standard for scientific evidence would be that it is "generally accepted by a typical cross-section of the relevant scientific community."

The tendency now, particularly in trials involving the rich or famous, is for both sides to hire as many expert witnesses as they think they will need to counter the other side's experts. The sight of dueling experts does not endear itself to a jury. As Francis Wellman said many years ago: "It has become a matter of common observation that not only can the honest opinions of different experts be obtained upon opposite sides of the same question, but also that dishonest opinions may be obtained upon different sides of the same question."[1]

In those solemn chambers where defense attorneys discuss the wisdom handed down from their distinguished predecessors, there is a saying repeated as a mantra and passed down to each fledgling

---

1. *Francis L. Wellman*, The Art of Cross-Examination.

attorney as part of her secret heritage: "If you've got a good case, hammer the evidence; if you have a weak one, hammer the People's witnesses; and if you have no case at all, hammer the prosecutors."

One way to hammer the prosecutor is to make his questioning seem ridiculous. One master of this technique was William Joseph Fallon, who dominated the New York criminal courtrooms during the first quarter of the twentieth century. While defending a larcenous young man named Peter "Petey the Kid" Regan, he objected strenuously to a series of questions the prosecutor asked his client on cross-examination, but the judge allowed them:

"Where were you in February 1908?" the prosecutor asked. "Where were you in January 1909?" and "Did you ever know 'English Harry'?" These, and many more questions in this vein, were aimed to show that Regan was flighty, and the friend of criminals.

Fallon stood up on redirect. "Petey, did you ever know any of the following persons: President Wilson? King George? Lillian Russell? Sir Oliver Lodge?"

The prosecution objected, and the judge upheld the objection. "It is unthinkable," the judge declared, "that such a manifestly foolish question be put by an attorney."

Fallon agreed. "Your Honor, that is the position I myself take. It is the position, if you will recall, I took a few minutes ago when the prosecution asked similar questions."

Fallon turned back to his client. "Petey, the prosecution has gone into exhaustive investigation of your alleged travels. Will you not tell me if you ever climbed the pyramids or slid down the Alps?"[2]

The laughter in the courtroom undid any good the prosecutor's questions had done. The jury was deadlocked. There was a second trial, and again the jury could not agree. The prosecution gave up and Regan was freed.

WOMEN IN COURT

Historically, the treatment of women in the courtroom, when it has not been to exclude them completely, has been to view them with great suspicion. The idea of a woman barrister was laughable through all the ages

---

2. *Dialog excerpted from* The Great Mouthpiece, *by Gene Fowler.*

of mankind until late in the present century. In the mid-eighteenth century, Samuel Johnson commented on the excitement engendered by a lady preacher: "A woman's preaching is like a dog's walking on its hinder legs. It is not done well; but you are surprised to find it done at all." He had no cause to comment on a woman lawyer, as there were none.

Women also seldom appeared as defendants in capital cases, and when they did the usual accusations were infanticide or witchcraft. Lesser crimes that brought women to the dock were shoplifting, prostitution, and "being a common scold." When a woman was tried for a crime, she was usually convicted; the conviction rate for women in New York State in the first half of the twentieth century was more than twice that of men. But this was a result of the insulation of women from the criminal system rather than the opposite: less than 10 percent of the defendants were women. A woman was not brought to trial unless she was clearly guilty and incorrigible.

Women were not commonly accepted as witnesses in criminal trials until well into the nineteenth century. In ancient Rome the testimony of women, although usually admitted, was barred in certain classes of trial. But women were much more equal in the Rome of the Caesars than in the Rome of the Popes. The civil canon laws of medieval Europe, as for example cited in the *Institutiones Juris Canonici* of Lancelottus, effectively barred women from testifying. As one medieval legal scribe (Mascardus) put it: "*Feminis plerumque omnino non creditur, et id dumtaxat, quod sunt feminæ quæ ut plurimum solent esse fraudulentæ fallaces, et dolosæ*" ("Generally speaking, no credence at all is given to women, and for this reason: because they are women, who are usually deceitful, untruthful, and treacherous in the very highest degree").

In Scotland, until the mid-eighteenth century a woman could be excluded from giving testimony because she was a woman. In Switzerland until the 1820s, the testimony of two women was required to counterbalance that of one man, although a virgin was to be given greater credence than a widow. The *Canonical Institutions of Devotus*, published in Paris in 1852, stated that, except in a few peculiar instances, women were not competent witnesses in criminal cases.

Rufus Choate, one of the greatest advocates of the nineteenth century, gave an associate the following advice:

> [N]ever cross-examine a woman. It's of no use. They cannot
> disintegrate the story they have once told. They cannot eliminate

the part that is for you from that which is against you. They can neither combine nor shade nor qualify. They go for the whole thing; and the moment you begin to cross-examine one of them, instead of being bitten by a single rattlesnake, you are bitten by a whole barrelful. I never, except in a case absolutely desperate, dare to cross-examine a woman.[3]

In his classic treatise *The Art of Cross-Examination*, first published in 1903, Francis Wellman suggests that in many cases it is just as well not to bother cross-examining a woman. Instead the attorney should:

Rise suddenly, as if you intended to cross-examine. The witness will turn a determined face toward you, prepared to demolish you with her first answer. This is the signal for you to hesitate a moment. Look her over good-naturedly and as if you were in doubt whether it would be worthwhile to question her—and sit down. It can be done by a good actor in such a manner as to be equivalent to saying to the jury, "What's the use? She is only a woman."

Women were generally excluded from juries until after World War II, when the states began gradually adding the names of women to the jury lists. It wasn't until 1955 that Texas allowed women to sit on juries.

Today these outdated notions have disappeared from American courtrooms, where female judges and attorneys regularly deal with female defendants and witnesses and address the women in juries. Attorneys of both sexes still have a sneaky feeling that there is a difference between men and women, but as to just what it is or how to deal with it on the witness stand, there is no consensus.

• • •

Artemus Porter developed his alternate theory of the crime with his next witnesses. Several people testified that to their knowledge, J.J. Johansohn regularly carried large sums of money with him. Porter also tried to introduce witnesses who would testify that Johansohn had been seen in the company of known underworld figures. He was trying to suggest the people known not to be averse to the notion of robbery with

---

3. *Quoted in Wellman.*

violence knew of this habit. But the judge would not allow this unless Porter could connect it up with direct evidence that could at least suggest the possibility that someone acted on this knowledge.

Porter introduced a garage attendant who testified that Lane's black Mercedes was in the garage all night the night of the murder. On cross-examination, Weiss was able to show that the attendant stayed in the office most of the night—since the regulars had their own gate passes—and Lane might have gone out without his knowledge.

HOSTILE WITNESSES

Porter then brought on a young man named Jack B. Quick and asked the judge to declare Quick a hostile witness. "We'll see how hostile he is," Judge Merkle said. "Go on with your examination."

* * *

A witness that has been called by one side in a court case is presumed to be hostile to the interests of the other side. Thus cross-examination is allowed greater leeway than direct examination. Leading questions, forbidden in direct examination, may be asked in cross. To be allowed the same latitude in direct examination, the examiner asks the judge to declare the witness as adverse or hostile. The witness so designated does not necessarily have knowledge of illicit or criminal acts; he could be a close friend of the defendant, hesitant to say anything nasty about him, or the owner or manager of a business who doesn't want anything detrimental to the business discussed in open court, or someone who has been threatened with bodily harm if he testifies, or someone who is just naturally hostile to the defense or the prosecution.

* * *

Porter took a while to get Quick to admit that he had been a lover of Lucille Lane's before J.J. Johansohn came into the picture. He tried to suggest that Quick was jealous, but got little help from Quick, who claimed that it was an enjoyable but casual relationship.

On cross-examination, Weiss brought out that Quick was now engaged to be married and had no reason to be jealous of anything that Lucille Lane might have done. A chance question did more damage to the defense.

Q: *While you were seeing Lucille Lane, did she ever express any opinion of her husband, Broderick?*

A: *She was scared to death of him.*

This was promptly objected to as hearsay, and the objection was sustained—but the damage had been done.

On that unfortunate note, the defense rested. Broderick Lane never took the stand. Perhaps it was because Porter was afraid he would lose his temper on cross-examination, perhaps there were some questions the prosecution might ask him for which he would not have a good answer, or perhaps he just wouldn't perform well on the stand. These are questions upon which we—and juries—are not supposed to speculate.

THE SECOND BITE

. . . nor shall any person be subject for the same offense to be twice put in jeopardy of life or limb . . .

—FROM THE FIFTH AMENDMENT TO THE CONSTITUTION OF THE UNITED STATES

In several prominent criminal cases this past decade the defendants have stood trial twice for the same offense, in apparent violation of the Fifth Amendment's bar to "double jeopardy." The brothers Lyle and Eric Menendez, accused of killing their parents, were tried twice in state court; the Los Angeles Police Department officers accused of beating Rodney King were tried once in state and once in federal court; O.J. Simpson, accused of killing his ex-wife Nicole Brown Simpson and her friend Ronald Goldman, was tried once in criminal court and once in civil court. In each case the defendants were found not guilty the first time and guilty (or, in Mr. Simpson's case, civilly liable) the second. Why in these cases was the Fifth Amendment not violated?

—In the case of the Menendez brothers, the second trial was the result of a hung jury (a jury unable to reach a verdict) in the first trial.

This was not a violation of the brothers' protection against "double jeopardy," as their jeopardy in the first trial had never been resolved. Had they been found innocent at the first trial, they could not have been retried. Indeed, had they been found guilty of a lesser offense, such as murder in the second degree, the prosecutor would not have been able to retry them to attempt to get a better verdict.

—Stacey Koon, Laurence Powell, and two other Los Angeles Police Department officers were acquitted of felony charges of assault with a deadly weapon and use of excessive force by a police officer in Simi Valley Superior Court for the beating of Rodney King, a black motorist whom they had apprehended after a high-speed chase. They were tried again in federal court, this time for willfully depriving King of his civil rights, a different offense subject to federal prosecution. And this time Koon and Powell were convicted. This may sound like legalistic hair-splitting, but the federal government has assumed the responsibility, and the authority, of retrying selected criminal cases involving murder or mayhem under the rubric of the civil rights statutes. This began in the 1960s, when it became clear that juries in some southern states were finding white men on trial for murdering black men or civil rights workers of any hue not guilty as a matter of course.

—Orenthal James Simpson was found not guilty of the murder of Nicole Brown Simpson and Ronald Goldman in a California criminal trial. Had he been found guilty, he could have gone to prison for life, as the prosecutor had decided not to ask for the death penalty. That was the jeopardy he was in, and once the jury brought in its verdict he could no longer be tried for the same offense in a criminal courtroom.

After the criminal trial, Fredric Goldman and Kimberly Erin Goldman, Ronald Goldman's father and sister, filed a Complaint for Damages for Wrongful Death, alleging that Simpson had "brutally murdered the decedent on June 12, 1994 at a location known as 875 South Bundy Drive." Louis H. Brown, Nicole Brown Simpson's father, asserted in a similar suit that Nicole had "died as the legal result of the wrongful acts of Orenthal James Simpson . . . ." The two suits were joined into one trial.

But a civil suit is not a criminal trial. A defendant is assured of freedom from double jeopardy in a criminal court, but not freedom from civil liability. If Mr. Simpson had been found guilty of murder, the relatives of the victims could have sued for damages; his having been found not guilty just made it more difficult for them to prove their case.

Because the stakes are not as high in a civil suit as in a criminal trial—the defendant can lose neither his life nor his liberty, but only money—the standards of proof are not as high. In a criminal trial the entire jury must agree that the defendant is guilty "beyond a reasonable doubt," which is the highest standard of proof in the law. In a civil trial, the jury must decide on the "preponderance of evidence." If one side convinces the jury of its story just a hair more than the other side, then that side wins. And a verdict does not have to be unanimous: in California, nine out of the twelve jurors will suffice.

Another difference between the civil and criminal trials was that in the civil trial, Mr. Simpson was obliged to testify. The Fifth Amendment protection against self-incrimination was moot since, Simpson having been found not guilty in the criminal trial, no further criminal prosecution of him was possible.

EIGHT

THE VERDICT

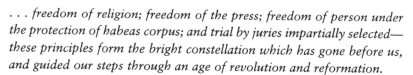

> . . . *freedom of religion; freedom of the press; freedom of person under the protection of habeas corpus; and trial by juries impartially selected—these principles form the bright constellation which has gone before us, and guided our steps through an age of revolution and reformation.*

— THOMAS JEFFERSON
FIRST INAUGURAL ADDRESS, MARCH 4, 1801

Artemus Porter gave his closing argument first, because the defense always summed up first in Arkham criminal courts. He spoke for a day and a half, giving his slant to every bit of evidence and every word of testimony. He savaged the idea of believing in circumstantial evidence. He chuckled over the prosecution's expert witness. He quoted from the Bible, the Book of Common Prayer, Shakespeare, Charles Dickens, and Bob Dylan. He spoke long and hard about "beyond a reasonable doubt." He told the jury that they had a duty to God and Country and Future Generations Yet Unborn to find his client innocent. He sat down.

Assistant D.A. Carter Weiss spoke for the rest of the second day and much of the third. He described circumstantial evidence as being the best sort of evidence, and reminded the jury how he had forged a chain of circumstances that, taken together, led to the inescapable conclusion that Broderick Lane had, with premeditation and malice aforethought, committed this dastardly crime. He reminded them of the two victims, who now had nobody but the state to speak for them. "You may feel pity for Broderick Lane, for he has done a horrible thing," he told them, "but you must also *feel pity for the victims, and you must do your duty to the people of the State of Arkham and find Broderick Lane guilty of two counts of murder in the first degree!" And Carter Weiss sat down.*

•   •   •

In most states, the party with the burden of proof—in criminal cases, the prosecution—give their closing argument last. In federal courts, and in a few states, the prosecution goes first and, often, is given a chance for a rebuttal argument after the defense give their closing argument. The prosecution, however, is not supposed to comment on the possible dishonesty of defense counsel, speak of evidence not in the trial record, or speculate as to why a defendant chose not to testify.

THE JUDGE'S CHARGE

Now came the judge's charge to the jury.

"You have heard all the evidence," Judge Merkle told them. "It is now my duty to instruct you as to the law that applies to this case." She spoke slowly and carefully for over an hour, and then sent the jury off to begin their deliberations.

•   •   •

If we may consider the jury as the official audience at a trial, whose task is to render the ultimate affirmation of one or another of the performers, then the last act belongs to the judge. His charge to the jury must be artfully crafted and carefully prepared. He must not allow his opinion as to the guilt or innocence of the defendant to color his remarks. He must tell the jurors the law relevant to the events of the trial, what they may consider, and what they must not consider. He may also inform them of such facts as:

- You must follow the law as I give it to you whether or not you agree with it.
- You must keep in mind that anything said by the attorneys is not evidence.
- You must evaluate the truth and importance of any testimony given by any witness based on your own common sense and experience.

In California, as in many other states, the form of certain jury instructions is fixed. Among these instructions, the juries in appropriate cases might hear:

- Murder is classified into two degrees, and if you should find the defendant guilty of murder, you must determine and state in your verdict whether you find the murder to be of the first or second degree.[1]
- Before you may return a verdict in this case, you must agree unanimously not only as to whether the defendant is guilty or not guilty, but also, if you should find [him/ her] guilty of an unlawful killing, you must agree unanimously as to whether [he/she] is guilty of [murder of the first degree] [or] [murder of the second degree] [or] [voluntary [or] involuntary manslaughter].
- If a human being is killed by any one of several persons engaged in the commission or attempted commission of the crime of _____, all persons, who either directly and actively commit the act constituting such crime, or who with knowledge of the unlawful purpose of the perpetrator of the crime and with the intent or purpose of committing, encouraging, or facilitating the commission of the offense, aid, promote, encourage, or instigate by act or advice its commission, are guilty of murder in the first degree, whether the killing is intentional, unintentional, or accidental.

• • •

After three days of deliberation, the jury returned its verdict. "Madam foreperson, have you reached a verdict?" Judge Merkle asked.

"We have, Your Honor," the foreperson answered. She handed the charge slip to the bailiff, who passed it to the judge. The judge glanced at it and passed it to the court clerk.

"Will the defendant please rise," the judge said. Broderick Lane and his attorney both rose.

"The clerk will now read the verdict," Judge Merkle instructed.

The clerk read: "In the case of the State of Arkham versus Broderick Lane for the unlawful death of Lucille Lane, a human being, a violation of Penal Code Section 136, we, the jury, find the defendant guilty of murder in the first degree. In the case

---

1. *Refer back to Chapter 3, p. 48, for what happens when the jury neglects to do this.*

*of the State of Arkham versus Broderick Lane for the unlawful death of J.J. Johansohn,
a human being, a violation of Penal Code Section 136, we, the jury, find the defendant guilty of murder in the first degree."*

UNTIL YOU ARE DEAD

*"Nothing in the social contract gives the state any right to take
human life."*

—CESARE DI BECCARIA, 1764

Capital punishment, that is, the killing by the state of specific individuals as a form of retribution, as differentiated from war, genocide, or rit-
ual murder, is at least as old as recorded history. In ancient Greece, the
ultimate punishment was banishment, to be sent into the barbarous
world outside, and to be forbidden contact with the motherland was
considered worse than death. But for the *hoi polloi*, too unsophisticat-
ed to appreciate the agony of such separation, death would suffice.

In Rome, in the fourth century B.C., ten specially selected men, the
Decemvirs, devised the Twelve Tables of the law, which remained the
basic law of Rome through the Republic, the Empire, and on for
the next 900 years. A set of laws as severe as the Roman aristocrats who
devised them, they decreed the death penalty for arson, bribery, perjury,
libel, stealing from a harvest, damaging crops, practicing magic, "sedi-
tious gatherings in the city by night," and murder. However, a citizen
could appeal his or her sentence to the "Assembly of Centuries," a sort
of lower house similar to our House of Representatives, or go into voluntary exile by just leaving Rome.

The Sanhedrin, the Hebrew court in ancient days, was meticulous in
preserving the rights of defendants in criminal trials. Capital cases were
particularly carefully considered. Prosecution witnesses were solemnly
informed of the seriousness of what they were doing, and people of low
morality were not allowed to testify for the prosecution, although anyone
could testify for the defense. The judges fasted for a day before sentencing
the offender. When an execution was scheduled, a rider was stationed
at the court ready to ride to halt the execution if new evidence showed
up. A crier went before the execution party shouting out the facts of the

crime and asking anyone who could speak in the condemned person's favor to come forward and do so. The condemned was permitted to stop four times on the way to the place of execution to plead his or her case. If all else failed, the Sanhedrin usually managed to find a technical legal reason why the execution should not be carried out, and the criminal's sentence would be commuted to life imprisonment.

In China during the Imperial period, punishment for criminal offenses came in five varieties: beating with a light bamboo stick, beating with a heavy bamboo stick, imprisonment, internal exile, and execution. The death penalty was further subdivided into strangulation, decapitation, and the death of a thousand slices. All death penalties were automatically reviewed by the Board of Punishments in Peking, looked at once more by a special body called the Three High Courts, and then sent for approval to the emperor. Somewhere along this process, most were reduced to a lower sentence, usually exile.[2]

Through the middle ages the crimes for which capital punishment was thought suitable expanded to include, at various times and places, heresy, witchcraft, piracy, brigandage, robbery, burglary, simple theft, purse-cutting, adultery, sodomy, rape, and treason. In eighteenth-century England there were over 200 hanging crimes, ranging from cutting down trees to stealing "more than 40 shillings worth of goods from a ship on a navigable river or wharf." By 1839, however, the number had gone down to 17. The past century has seen the use of capital punishment as a tool of civic management disappear from much of the world; some of the nations abolishing it have been:

1863: Belgium
1867: Portugal
1870: The Netherlands*
1882: Brazil*
1895: Ecuador
1905: Norway
1910: Colombia
1921: Argentina*, Sweden
1926: Costa Rica, Peru, Uruguay, Venezuela
1930: Chile
1932: Spain

---

2. *Imperial Chinese authorities had wonderful flexibility in dealing with crime. One statute punishing violators of imperial decrees was also applied to acts that the emperor would have forbidden, had he thought of them.*

1933: Denmark
1941: New Zealand
1975: Mexico
1976: Canada
1977: Portugal
1978: Spain
1979: Brazil*, Fiji, Luxembourg, Nicaragua, Norway
1980: Peru
1981: France
1982: The Netherlands*
1983: Cyprus, El Salvador
1984: Argentina*, Australia

The asterisked countries reinstated capital punishment, usually under authoritarian regimes, and then eliminated it again.

A few countries today use the death penalty for only the most heinous of crimes. In Israel it is reserved for "Crimes Against Humanity," and, despite continuous provocation, it has been used only once in the half-century of Israel's existence.

The United States is alone among Western democracies today in a continuing rush to execute. Our only competition in the death penalty derby comes from regressive authoritarian states. In 1995, the government of Saudi Arabia beheaded 192 people, most of them convicted for smuggling drugs. The country's beheadings in 1996 included four Saudis involved in the bombing of a U.S. installation that killed four Americans and two Indians. Punishment came so hard on the heels of judgment that American investigators never got a chance to question the four.

In mid-1996, in a campaign called Yanda ("strike hard"), the government of the People's Republic of China conducted a vast program of arresting, trying, and executing "criminals," with the entire process from arrest to firing squad sometimes taking no more than three days. Amnesty International has confirmed that a thousand people were executed and fears that the true number is far higher.

CAPITAL PUNISHMENT

A week later, the court convened again for the jury to consider the last phase of the trial—the question of special circumstances. In this case the prosecutor alleged two special circumstances: multiple murder and murder for gain. If the jury agreed, the judge would have to invoke the death sentence.

The defense attorney presented evidence in mitigation, introducing witnesses to show Lane as a good person, and useful to the community. Lane's aged mother took the stand to plead for her son's life. As Lane was still not admitting the killing, the defense felt itself precluded from introducing the possible provocation of Lucille's behavior. Porter did stress the possibility that the jury might someday discover that it had been mistaken in its verdict, and it would be hard to apologize to Lane if he had been executed. "Let the doubts that remain in your heart as to Broderick Lane's guilt, however slight they may be, dictate this final decision you must make," he pleaded.

One week and one day later the jury found that the special circumstances existed, and Broderick Lane was sentenced to death by lethal injection, Arkham's current way of inflicting the supreme punishment.

Lane is still on death row, as his appeals are working their way through the court system. The betting by those knowledgeable about such matters is that one of his appeals will get him a new trial, or that the court will reduce the verdict to life imprisonment, that in any case he will certainly not be executed, and that he will probably be released in a reasonable length of time. This is not based on any known flaw in the trial, but on the fact that no man or woman of wealth has ever been executed in the United States.

AGGRAVATION v MITIGATION

After finding Timothy McVeigh guilty of the bombing of the Federal Building in Oklahoma City, and the resulting murder of 168 people, the jury in his trial in Denver on federal murder charges then separately had to decide whether they should recommend the death penalty. Although the federal statute describes it as a "recommendation" the judge could not impose the death sentence without the jury's recommendation, and there was little chance that the judge would go against the jury if it did so recommend. On Friday, June 13, 1997, it brought in its decision.

The jury worked from a questionnaire, and found as follows:

Intent to Cause Death:
Each of these points needed a unanimous yes vote for the jury to recommend that the death penalty to be applied:
   1. The defendant intentionally killed the victims. *[Unanimous yes]*

2. The defendant intentionally inflicted serious body injury that resulted in the death of the victims. *[Unanimous yes]*

3. The defendant intentionally participated in an act, contemplating that the life of a person would be taken or intending that lethal force would be used against a person, and the victims died as a result of that act. *[Unanimous yes]*

4. The defendant intentionally and specifically engaged in an act of violence, knowing that the act created a grave risk of death to a person, other than a participant in the offense, such that participation in the act constituted a reckless disregard for human life and the victims died as a direct result of the act. *[Unanimous yes]*

If all the above were unanimous, the jury had to balance the aggravating factors listed below against the mitigating factors listed below. Only if the aggravating factors outweighed the mitigating factors could the death penalty be recommended.

Aggravating Factors
Statutory (Specified in Federal Law):

1. The deaths or injuries resulting in death occurred during the commission of an offense under 18 United States Code Section 844(d), transportation of explosives in interstate commerce for certain purposes. *[Unanimous yes]*

2. The defendant, in the commission of the offenses, knowingly created a grave risk of death to one or more persons in addition to the victims of the offense. *[Unanimous yes]*

3. The defendant committed the offenses after substantial planning and premeditation to cause the death of one or more persons and to commit an act of terrorism. *[Unanimous yes]*

4. The defendant committed the offenses against one or more federal law enforcement officers because of such victims' status as federal law enforcement officers. *[Unanimous yes]*

Non-statutory (Approved by the Judge):

1. The offenses committed by the defendant resulted in the deaths of 168 persons. *[Unanimous yes]*

2. In committing the offenses, the defendant caused serious physical and emotional injury, including maiming, disfigurement, and permanent disability to numerous individuals. *[Unanimous yes]*

3. That by committing the offenses, the defendant caused severe injuries and losses suffered by the victims' families. *[Unanimous yes]*

Mitigating Factors

These are suggested by the defense attorney, but the jury is free to consider whatever it wishes in mitigation.

1. Timothy McVeigh believed deeply in the ideals upon which the United States was founded. *[Unanimous no]*
2. Timothy McVeigh believed that the ATF and FBI were responsible for the deaths of everyone who lost their lives at Mt. Carmel, near Waco, Texas, between February 28 and April 19, 1993. *[Unanimous yes]*
3. Timothy McVeigh believed that federal law enforcement agents murdered Sammy Weaver and Vicki Weaver near Ruby Ridge, Idaho, in August, 1992. *[Unanimous yes]*
4. Timothy McVeigh believed that the increasing use of military-style force and tactics by federal law enforcement agencies against American citizens threatened an approaching police state. *[Unanimous yes]*
5. Timothy McVeigh's belief that federal law enforcement agencies failed to take responsibilities for their actions at Ruby Ridge and Waco and failed to punish those persons responsible added to his growing concerns regarding the existence of a police state and a loss of constitutional liberties. *[Unanimous yes]*
6. Timothy McVeigh served honorably and with great distinction in the United States Army from May, 1988, until December, 1991. *[10 yes, 2 no]*
7. Timothy McVeigh received the Army's Bronze Star for his heroic service in operation Desert Storm in Kuwait and Iraq. *[Unanimous yes]*
8. Timothy McVeigh is a reliable and dependable person in work and in his personal affairs and relations with others. *[2 yes, 10 no]*
9. Timothy McVeigh is a person who deals honestly with others in interpersonal relations. *[1 yes, 11 no]*
10. Timothy McVeigh is a patient and effective teacher when he is working in a supervisory role. *[Unanimous yes]*
11. Timothy McVeigh is a good and loyal friend. *[Unanimous no]*
12. Over the course of his life, Timothy McVeigh has done good deeds for and helped others, including a number of strangers who needed assistance. *[4 yes, 8 no]*

13. Timothy McVeigh has no prior criminal record. *[Unanimous yes]*

The jurors were also provided with extra spaces to write in additional mitigating factors, if any, found by any one or more jurors. *[None were found]*

Recommendation

The jury has considered whether the aggravating factors found to exist sufficiently outweigh any mitigating factor or factors found to exist, or in the absence of any mitigating factors, whether the aggravating factors are themselves sufficient to justify a sentence of death. Based upon this consideration, the jury recommends by unanimous vote that the following sentence be imposed:
The defendant, Timothy James McVeigh, shall be sentenced to death.

Certification

Each juror certifies by his or her signature that consideration of the race, color, religious beliefs, national origin, or sex of the defendant or the victims was not involved in reaching his or her individual decision and that the individual juror would have made the same recommendation regarding a sentence for the crimes in question no matter what the race, color, religious beliefs, national origin, or sex of the defendant or the victims.

As we entered 1997, 20 years after the end of the brief Supreme Court–imposed hiatus in the death sentence, there were over 3,100 people on the various death rows throughout the United States. From 1977, when the hiatus ended, through 1995 there were 314 people executed, 56 of them in 1995. As this chart, based on information from Amnesty International, shows, the number goes ever upward:

1976: 0	1986: 18
1977: 1	1987: 25
1978: 1	1988: 11
1979: 2	1989: 16
1980: 0	1990: 23
1981: 1	1991: 14
1982: 2	1992: 31
1983: 5	1993: 38
1984: 21	1994: 31
1985: 18	1995: 56

This total was achieved by 179 lethal injections, 123 electrocutions, nine trips to the gas chamber, two hangings, and one firing squad.

The American belief in the efficacy of capital punishment dates from the founding of the colonies. The God-fearing Puritans who settled Massachusetts came from an England that had over 200 offenses meriting the death penalty, but they took it in directions never imagined in their homeland. The Puritans based their laws on the Bible, and they found biblical sanction for an extended use of the death penalty. The Laws and Liberties of Massachusetts of 1648, in a section called "Capitall Lawes," invoked the death sentence for a number of crimes, citing the appropriate biblical passage for each, *viz*: "If any person slayeth another suddenly in his ANGER, or CRUELTY of passion, he shall be put to death. Levit. 24.17. Numb. 35.20.21." In addition to murder, blasphemy, buggery, idolatry, adultery, and witchcraft were proscribed, as well as the return of Quakers to the colony after having been banished. If a man committed the "unnatural & horrid act of Bestiallitie" upon an animal, both the man and the animal could be put to death.

Adultery was not a capital offense back in England, but the Puritan lawmakers were of sterner stuff. The law shortly fell into disuse because it was found that juries, when actually faced with the prospect of hanging a couple for adultery, usually backed down and refused to convict.

The number of offenses for which the death penalty was considered appropriate decreased through the eighteenth and nineteenth centuries, but the absolute number of people executed per year crept slowly upward. The peak to date was reached in 1935, when 199 people were put to death in the United States. Compare this to the 155 people who were executed over the entire decade of 1890–1900.

CRUEL AND UNUSUAL

Excessive bail shall not be required, nor excessive fines imposed, nor cruel and unusual punishments inflicted.

—Eighth Amendment to the United States Constitution

In 1972, in a case known as *Furman v Georgia*, the Supreme Court decided that the death penalty, as practiced by the various states at that time, comprised punishment that was sufficiently cruel and unusual as to be unconstitutional. By a five-to-four vote it reversed three death penalty decisions, holding that "the imposition and carrying out of the death penalty in these cases constitutes cruel and unusual punishment in violation of the Eighth and Fourteenth Amendments." The decision actually joined three appeals, *Furman v Georgia*, *Jackson v Georgia*, and *Branch v Texas*, in which three defendants, all black men, had been sentenced to death, one for murder and two for rape. The majority opinion seemed to say that while capital punishment was, in itself, not unconstitutional, the manner in which it was being applied was arbitrary and capricious, and thus in violation of the Eighth Amendment's ban on cruel and unusual punishment.

The "due process" clause of the Fourteenth Amendment (*"No state shall make or enforce any law which shall abridge the privileges or immunities of citizens of the United States; nor shall any state deprive any person of life, liberty, or property, without due process of law; nor deny to any person within its jurisdiction the equal protection of the laws."*) was added to the Constitution after the Civil War. In a gradual process beginning in the 1930s, the Fourteenth Amendment was seen by the Supreme Court as extending the Constitution's protections for individuals to the actions of the states, where previously these protections had been applied only to actions of the federal government.

The closeness of the vote and the fact that each of the nine justices felt it necessary to write a separate opinion made it seem probable to the attorneys who studied the decision that the question of the constitutionality of capital punishment was not yet closed. Only two of the justices, Brennan and Marshall, stated unequivocally that the Eighth Amendment should constitute a total bar to capital punishment. Justice Douglas came close, but seemed to hedge a little on the idea of an absolute ban. Justice Stewart wrote that the arguments of his fellow justices against the death penalty were compelling, but Supreme Court justices break new constitutional ground very cautiously, and he didn't see the need to go quite so far in deciding this case.

In his separate opinion making fairness the issue, Justice Douglas affirmed this broadening of the coverage of the Eighth Amendment, quoting from an earlier decision that the amendment "must draw its meaning from the evolving standards of decency that mark the progress of a maturing society."[3] He concluded, "It would seem to be incontestable that the death penalty inflicted on one defendant is 'unusual' if it discriminates against him by reason of his race, religion, wealth, social position, or class, or if it is imposed under a procedure that gives room for the play of such prejudices."

In concurring, Justice Brennan reviewed the history of the death penalty and wrote that "the true significance of these punishments is that they treat members of the human race as nonhumans, as objects to be toyed with and discarded."

Justice Marshall traced the history of the concept of "cruel and unusual punishments" from seventeenth-century England to the twentieth-century United States. He examined six reasons that a state might want to invoke capital punishment: "retribution, deterrence, prevention of repetitive criminal acts, encouragement of guilty pleas and confessions, eugenics, and economy." After carefully and conscientiously examining each of these reasons, he came to the conclusion that none of them was valid, and that "the death penalty is an excessive and unnecessary punishment that violates the Eighth Amendment."

Chief Justice Burger, in his dissent to the majority opinion, wrote that he personally agreed with Justices Brennan and Marshall, and would "at the very least, restrict the use of capital punishment to a small category of the most heinous crimes." But he felt that the court's inquiry "must be divorced from personal feelings as to the morality and efficacy of the death penalty, and be confined to the meaning and applicability of the uncertain language of the Eighth Amendment." His conclusion was that "cruel and unusual" did not prohibit capital punishment, and that to do so would be a job for the legislature, not the courts.

Justice Blackmun, after affirming "I yield to no one in the depth of my distaste, antipathy, and, indeed, abhorrence, for the death penalty," and that he believed it served no useful purpose, nevertheless went along with Chief Justice Burger in opining that it wasn't the Supreme Court's job to end it.

The *Furman* decision did not bar capital punishment, just certain ways of applying it. Its immediate effect was to end executions in the United States and cause the sentences of those on the thirty-odd death rows to be commuted to life imprisonment, as no state's existing death penalty procedures would comply with what the Supreme Court seemed to be asking.

---

3. *Trop v Dulles.*

After a few years of jockeying and experimentation, those states that wanted to reinstate the death penalty had examined *Furman's* implications and arrived at a formula that they believed would pass the Supreme Court's scrutiny and allow them to put their gallows, electric chairs, and gas chambers back on line. Within three years of the *Furman* decision, the legislatures of 35 states had passed new death penalty laws. In order to be "death eligible"—a wonderful phrase—the defendant had to be convicted of murder in the first degree with special circumstances, which varied slightly from state to state. The California statute included murder for financial gain; multiple murders; murder of police officers or firefighters; murder of witnesses, prosecutors, or judges; "hate crimes" in which the victim was killed because of his or her color, race, religion, or nationality; and murders that were "especially heinous, atrocious or cruel, manifesting exceptional depravity."

If the defendant is convicted of a "special circumstance" murder, then the penalty phase, a sort of second trial, is held, in California with the same jury and in some states with only the judge. In this phase, the jury or judge must consider "aggravating and mitigating factors" and decide whether to impose the death penalty. Aggravating factors might include the circumstances surrounding the murder and other violent criminal activity of the defendant, whether committed before or after the murder. Mitigating factors might include the defendant's age, mental state, and degree of participation in the crime (was she a principal or merely an accomplice?), or any other factor the defense attorney thinks might sway the jury. Although what can be included as an aggravating factor by the prosecution is, in most states, specified by statute, the defense may bring into evidence anything it considers helpful. As Chief Justice Burger said, writing for the plurality in a 1978 decision (*Lockett v Ohio*):

> [W]e conclude that the Eighth and Fourteenth Amendments require that the sentencer . . . not be precluded from considering, as a mitigating factor, *any aspect of a defendant's character or record and any of the circumstances of the offense that the defendant proffers as a basis for a sentence less than death.* (Emphasis in the original.)

The jury must decide whether the aggravating factors outweigh the mitigating factors, in which case it may vote for death, or whether the mitigating factors outweigh the aggravating factors, in which case the defendant serves life in prison.

The Texas legislature devised three questions for the jury to answer, which, stripped of legalese could be stated as:

- Did the defendant commit his murder deliberately and with the expectation that the victim or anyone else would die?
- Is there a probability that the defendant would constitute a continuing threat to society, and
- Was the conduct of the defendant an unreasonable response to provocation by the victim, if there was such provocation?

If the jury unanimously answers "yes" to each of the questions, the trial judge must sentence the defendant to death. The defense attorney is free to bring in any evidence in mitigation that she can to direct the jury's mind to a "no" answer to any one of these questions.

It took some time for the capital cases prosecuted under the new understanding to wend their way through the judicial system, and it was not until 1979, after *Furman*, that executions resumed under the new rules. They are now presumed to be no longer cruel and, in some states, such as Florida and Texas, certainly not unusual.

APPENDIX

Complete List of Questions for Potential Jurors in the Trial of O.J. Simpson for the Murder of Nicole Brown Simpson and Ronald Goldman 9/30/94.

I. FAMILY HISTORY—BACKGROUND

1. Age?
2. Are you male or female?
3. What is your race? (please circle)
    a. White/Caucasian?
    b. Black/African-American?
    c. Hispanic/Latino?
    d. Asian/Pacific Islander?
    e. Other (please state)?
4. Marital status:
    ___ Single and never married?
    ___ Single, but living with non-marital mate. For how long?
    ___ Currently married? Length of marriage?
    ___ Divorced? When divorced? Length of previous marriage? Did you initiate the divorce? Yes? No?
    ___ Widowed? Length of marriage?

5. If you have children, please list (include children not living with you): Sex? Age? Does child live with you? Level of education? Occupation?

6. Do you have grown grandchildren? Yes? No? If yes: Sex? Age? Occupation?

7. Do you have a medical or physical condition that might make it difficult for you to serve as a juror? (Please include any hearing or eyesight problem or difficulty in climbing stairs.) No? Yes? Please describe.

8. Are you presently taking any form of medication? If so, please list the medications you are taking, the reasons for taking them and how often you take them.

9. Do you have any problems or areas of concern at home or at work that might interfere with your duties as a juror during trial? Yes? No? If yes, please describe.

II. RESIDENTIAL HISTORY

10. What part of Los Angeles County do you currently live in and what is your postal Zip Code? (If you live in the City of Los Angeles please specify the area, for example: South Central, Crenshaw.) Zip Code?

11. How long have you lived at your present residence?

12. Which of the following best describes your current type of residence? Rental apartment? Own home? Rental house? Rental (other)? Other (specify)? Own apartment or condo? Own mobile home?

13. List areas of past residence within the last ten years and indicate how long you lived in each location.

14. Where were you born?

15. Where were you raised?

16. Is English your first language? Yes? No? If no, what is your first language?

17. Do you speak any language other than English? Yes? What language(s)? No?

18. Do you have any difficulty:

    —Reading English? Yes? Sometimes? No?

    —Understanding spoken English? Yes? Sometimes? No?

III. EMPLOYMENT

19. Are you currently employed outside the home? Yes? No? If so, by whom are you employed? Full or part time? If part time, how many hours per week? How long have you been so employed?

20. What are your specific duties and responsibilities on the job?

21. Does your job involve management or supervisory duties? Yes? No? If your answer is yes, please describe your managerial responsibilities and state the number of employees you supervise.

22. Do you have the authority to hire and fire employees? Yes? No? If yes, is this a difficult decision to make? Yes? No? Please explain.

23. If not currently employed outside the home, please check the category that applies to your employment status: Homemaker? Unemployed—looking for work? Unemployed—not looking for work? Student? Retired? Disabled?

24. If you are not currently employed outside the home but were previously so employed, please describe your most recent form of employment, stating the name of your employer, whether you were employed full or part time, when and for how long you were so employed.

25. Please list your work experience over the past ten years and state when and for how long you were employed at each job. Please give a brief description of each job and the name of each employer. If additional space is needed please use the blank pages provided at the back of the questionnaire and put the number of this question next to your answer.

26. Have you ever worked in the entertainment industry in any capacity? No? Yes? If yes, please explain.

27. Do you have any close friends or relatives who either have worked in the past or are currently working in any capacity in the entertainment industry? No? Yes? If yes, please indicate what relation s-he is to you and where s-he is or was so employed.

28. Have you ever worked in journalism or the news industry in any capacity? No? Yes? If yes, please state where and when you were so employed and give a brief description of your duties.

29. Do you have any close friends or relatives who either have worked or are currently working in journalism or in the news industry in any capacity? No? Yes? If yes, please state where and when s-he was so employed and give a brief description of his or her duties.

30. Have you ever worked in a laboratory or in any medical research or testing facility? No? Yes? If yes, please describe your duties and when and for how long you were so employed.

IV. EDUCATION

31. What is the last level of education you completed?

    ___ Grade school or less? Please circle one: 1–2–3–4–5–6.

    ___ Junior High School? Please circle one: 7–8–9.

    ___ High School? Please circle one: 10–11–12.

    ___ Technical, Vocational or Business school?

    For the above answers, please indicate number of years attended, field of study and any degrees achieved.

    ___ College? Please circle one: 13–14–15–16.

    Please indicate the degree(s) achieved, if any.

    ___ Post graduate work? Please indicate degree achieved.

32. If you attended one or more high schools for any length of time, please give the name of each high school and the city in which each is located.

33. If you attended any schools or colleges after high school, please name the schools and colleges you attended, your major areas of study, and the field in which you obtained your degree(s).

34. Please name any other educational programs you have attended (vocational schools, certification programs, part-time study).

35. Are you currently in school? Yes? No? If yes, which school and what are you studying?

36. Do you plan to attend school in the future? Yes? No? If yes, where do you plan to go and what do you plan to study?

37. What special training or skills do you have? (Please include any technical, medical, psychology or scientific training and special skills acquired on the job.)

38. Do you have any legal training or have you taken any law course? Yes? No? If yes, please explain.

39. While in school, what was your favorite subject?

40. What was your least favorite subject?

V. MILITARY

41. Have you ever served in the military? Yes? No? If yes, please list: Branch of service, Rank, Dates of service.

42. Combat experience? Yes? No? If yes, please explain.

43. Were you ever involved in any way with military law enforcement, court martial or investigations? Yes? No? If yes, please explain.

44. While serving in the military, did you ever see one or more people who were seriously wounded? Yes? No? If yes, please describe.

45. While serving in the military, did you ever see someone being killed or who had been killed? Yes? No? If yes, please describe.

46. Was your spouse or significant other ever in the military? Yes? No? If yes, what branch and when?

47. Were you involved with your spouse or significant other when s-he was in the military? Yes? No? Has your spouse or significant other's military experience affected you? Yes? No? If yes, please describe how.

VI. YOUR SPOUSE OR PARTNER'S BACKGROUND

48. Please complete regarding your current spouse or partner: If he or she is (please check): widowed, divorced, separated. Please complete all of the following questions regarding your spouse/mate:

49. Spouse/partner's place of birth?

50. Spouse/partner's race or ethnic background?

51. Spouse/partner's current employment status?

52. What is that person's occupation? (If that person is retired, unemployed or disabled, what was his/her occupation?)

53. By whom is he or she employed?

54. How long has he or she worked there?

55. What is the last level of education s-he completed and please list any degrees s-he has?

VII. PARENTS AND SIBLINGS

56. What are/were your parents' (and/or step-parents') occupations? (If retired or deceased, what did they do?) Mother, Father, Step-Mother, Step-Father.

57. Do you have any brothers or sisters with whom you were raised? Yes? No? If yes, please list: Sex, Age, Relationship to you, Occupation.

VIII. LEGAL-COURTROOM EXPERIENCE

58. Have you, or any member of the family, or any close friend ever been arrested? Yes? No? If yes, who and how many times?

59. For each arrest, please describe what the charge(s) was, whether there was a jury trial, and what the outcome was.

60. Other than as a potential juror or for a case which you had been arrested, have you ever been in a courtroom for any other reason? Yes? No? If yes, how many times and for what purpose(s)?

61. Have you or any family members or close friends ever sued or been sued in a civil action? Yes? No? If yes, how many times? If yes, please explain the nature of the dispute.

62. Have you ever served on a jury before? Yes? No? For each time you have sat on a jury, please indicate the type of case, when you served, whether a verdict was reached, and, if no verdict was reached, the reason. Please do NOT state the verdict:

    Example: civil—car accident, 1984, yes.

    Example: criminal—robbery, 1986, no—deadlocked.

    Example: criminal—assault: 1992, no—case settled.

    Type of case, Year, Was a verdict reached? (Please do NOT state the verdict.)

63. Have you ever served on a grand jury? Yes? No? If yes, was it state or federal and when was it?

64. Have you ever sat on a coroner's jury? Yes? No? If yes, when and where?

65. Have you ever been the foreperson of a jury? Yes? No? If yes, please state what type of case and when.

66. Was a verdict reached in that case(s)? (Please do NOT state the verdict.) If not, why not?

67. How do you feel about your prior jury experience?

68. Please state your personal belief regarding each statement:

    A. "A defendant is innocent until proven guilty beyond a reasonable doubt." Strongly agree? Agree? Disagree strongly? Disagree? No opinion?

B. "If the prosecution goes to the trouble of bringing someone to trial, the person is probably guilty." Strongly disagree? Agree? Strongly disagree? Disagree? No opinion?

C. "The testimony of law enforcement officers or agents is not entitled to any greater or lesser weight merely because they are law enforcement officers or agents." Strongly agree? Agree? Strongly disagree? Disagree? No opinion?

D. "Regardless of what the law says, a defendant in a criminal trial should be required to prove his or her innocence." Strongly agree? Agree? Strongly disagree? Disagree? No opinion?

E. "People who make a lot of money are treated better by our court system than other people." Strongly agree? Agree? Strongly disagree? Disagree? No opinion?

69. Do you believe that a defendant in a criminal case should testify or produce some evidence to prove that he or she is not guilty? Yes? No? If yes, please explain why.

70. If selected as a juror in this case, the Court will instruct you as follows:

"You must not be influenced by pity for a defendant or by prejudice against him. You must not be biased against the defendant because he has been arrested for this offense, charged with a crime, or brought to trial. None of these circumstances is evidence of guilt and you must not infer or assume from any or all of them that he is more likely to be guilty or innocent. You must not be influenced by mere sentiment, conjecture, sympathy, passion, prejudice, public opinion, or public feeling. Both the People and the defendant have a right to expect that you will conscientiously consider and weigh the evidence, apply the law, and reach a just verdict regardless of the consequences." Are you willing to follow this instruction? Yes? No?

71. If selected as a juror in this case, the Court will instruct you as follows:

"A defendant in a criminal action is presumed to be innocent until the contrary is proved, and in case of a reasonable doubt whether his guilt is satisfactorily shown, he is entitled to a verdict of not guilty. This presumption places upon the People the burden of proving him guilty beyond a reasonable doubt.

"Reasonable doubt is defined as follows: It is not a mere possible doubt; because everything relating to human affairs, and depending on moral evidence, is open to some possible or imaginary doubt. It is that state of the case which, after the entire comparison and consideration of all the evidence, leaves the minds of the jurors in that condition that they cannot say they feel an abiding conviction, to a moral certainty, of the truth of the charge."

Are you willing to follow this instruction? Yes? No?

72. Why do you feel that you would be a good juror for this case?

73. Knowing what you know about this case thus far, do you want to be a juror in this case?

74. As part of your service on this case, the Court will order you not to read, listen to, or watch any accounts of this case reported by television, radio, or other news media. Will you have any difficulty following this order? Yes? No? Do not know?

75. If you are selected as a trial juror in this case the Court will order you not to discuss this case with ANYONE unless and until permitted to do so by the Court. Will you have any difficulty in following this order? Yes? No? Do not know?

76. If you are selected as a trial juror in this case, the Court will order that you not request, accept, agree to accept or discuss with any person receiving or accepting, any payment or benefit in consideration for supplying any information regarding this trial. Will you have any difficulty following this order? Yes? No? Do not know?

77. You will be required to sign an acknowledgment and agreement to abide by the Court's orders contained in items 74, 75 and 76 above. Will you have any difficulty signing and accepting these orders? Yes? No? Do not know?

IX. MEDIA COVERAGE

78. Because this case has received extensive publicity many, if not all, of you will have heard and/or read something about this case at some time. It is vitally important that you truthfully answer the following questions concerning what you have learned about this case from the media. There are no right or wrong answers. There should only be truthful and forthright answers.

Please indicate from what sources you have learned about this case (check as many as apply): Television? Newspapers? Radio? Magazines? Books? Tabloids? Have had conversations with other people? Have overheard other people discuss it? Other (please specify)?

79. Please rank the following sources of information by placing a number 1 next to the source from which you received the most information about the case; a number 2 next to the source from which you received the second most amount of information about the case, etc. Television? Newspapers? Radio? Magazines? Books? Tabloids? Have had conversations with other people? Have overheard other people discuss it? Other (please specify)?

80. If you have learned about this case from television, radio, newspapers, or magazines, please check all areas listed below which describe your exposure to each:

Television:

KNXT News, Ch. 2? Regularly? Sometimes? Seldom? Never?

KNBC News, Ch. 4? Regularly? Sometimes? Seldom? Never?

KTLA News, Ch. 5? Regularly? Sometimes? Seldom? Never?

KABC News, Ch. 7? Regularly? Sometimes? Seldom? Never?

KCAL News, Ch. 9? Regularly? Sometimes? Seldom? Never?

FOX News, Ch. 11? Regularly? Sometimes? Seldom? Never?

CNN (Cable News Network)? Regularly? Sometimes? Seldom? Never?

KCET News? Regularly? Sometimes? Seldom? Never?

Court T.V.? Regularly? Sometimes? Seldom? Never?

Other? Regularly? Sometimes? Seldom? Never?

Radio:

KFI Radio AM 640? Regularly? Sometimes? Seldom? Never?

KABC Radio AM 790? Regularly? Sometimes? Seldom? Never?

KFWB Radio AM 980? Regularly? Sometimes? Seldom? Never?

KCRW Radio FM 89.9? Regularly? Sometimes? Seldom? Never?

KNX Radio AM 1070? Regularly? Sometimes? Seldom? Never?

Other? Regularly? Sometimes? Seldom? Never?

Newspapers:

Los Angeles Times? Regularly? Sometimes? Seldom? Never?

The Daily News? Regularly? Sometimes? Seldom? Never?

Los Angeles Sentinel? Regularly? Sometimes? Seldom? Never?

USA Today? Regularly? Sometimes? Seldom? Never?

The Daily Journal? Regularly? Sometimes? Seldom? Never?

Other? Regularly? Sometimes? Seldom? Never?

Magazines:

Newsweek? Regularly? Sometimes? Seldom? Never?

Time? Regularly? Sometimes? Seldom? Never?

People? Regularly? Sometimes? Seldom? Never?

Los Angeles Magazine? Regularly? Sometimes? Seldom? Never?

The New Yorker? Regularly? Sometimes? Seldom? Never?

Other (please specify)? Regularly? Sometimes? Seldom? Never?

Tabloids:

The National Enquirer? Regularly? Sometimes? Seldom? Never?

The National Examiner? Regularly? Sometimes? Seldom? Never?

The Globe? Regularly? Sometimes? Seldom? Never?

Star? Regularly? Sometimes? Seldom? Never?

Other? Regularly? Sometimes? Seldom? Never?

The preliminary hearing on this case was broadcast live on both radio and television from June 30, 1994 through July 8, 1994.

81. Did you watch any portion of the preliminary hearing on television? Yes? No? If yes, how many days of the total 7 days of the preliminary hearing did you watch at least some portion of the hearing on television? Days? If yes, how many hours per day, on average, did you watch the hearing? Hours per day, on average?

82. The witnesses listed below testified at the preliminary hearing. Please check the witnesses you recall and describe your impression of each.

Allen Wattenberg (owner of the knife store)?

Jose Camacho (knife store salesman)?

John De Bello (restaurant manager)?

Karen Crawford (restaurant bar manager)?

Stewart Tanner (waiter)?

Pablo Fenjves (neighbor)?

Steven Schwab (dog owner & neighbor)?

Sukru Boztepe (neighbor)?

Bettina Rasmussen (neighbor) (Sukru Boztepe's wife)?

Allan Park (limousine driver)?

Brian "Kato" Kaelin?

Rachel Ferrara (Kato's friend)?

LAPD Detective Philip Vannatter?

LAPD Detective Mark Fuhrman?

Arnelle Simpson?

Dennis Fung (criminalist)?

LAPD Detective Tom Lange?

Thano Peratis (nurse)?

Greg Matheson (criminalist)?

Dr. Irwin Golden (coroner)?

Additional Comments?

83. Did you listen to any portion of the preliminary hearing on the radio? Yes? No? If yes, how many days of the 7 days of the preliminary hearing did you listen to at least some portion of it on the radio? Days? If yes, how many hours per day, on average, did you listen to the preliminary hearing on the radio? Hours per day, on average?

84. Please describe the witnesses and nature of the testimony which you recall hearing on the radio.

85. If you are selected to serve as a juror in this case, the court will instruct you as follows: "You must decide all questions of fact in this case from the evidence received in this trial and not from any other source." Are you willing to follow this instruction? Yes? No?

86. Please describe your impression concerning the lawyers for O.J. Simpson: Robert Shapiro? Johnnie Cochran? Gerald Uelman? Alan Dershowitz? Robert Kardashian? F. Lee Bailey?

87. Please describe your impression concerning the lawyers for the people of the State of California: Marcia Clark? William Hodgman?

88. Have you seen television coverage, other than appearances in court, of any of the lawyers for the defense? Yes? No? If yes, please describe what you recall, and which defense lawyer you observed. If yes, what was your reaction to what you observed? Please specify the defense lawyer to whom you are referring.

89. Have you observed television coverage, other than appearances in court, of any of the lawyers for the prosecution? Yes? No? If yes, please describe what you recall, and which prosecution lawyer you observed. If yes, what was your reaction to what you observed? Please specify the prosecution lawyer to whom you are referring.

90. Have you watched on television or listened on the radio to live coverage of any portion of the other hearings which have been held since the preliminary hearing ended on July 8? Yes? No? If yes, what do you recall about those hearings?

91. Which of the following best describes how you would describe the media coverage overall? Accurate? Sometimes accurate—Sometimes not? Inaccurate?

92. Which of the following best describes how you would describe the media coverage overall? Biased in favor of the prosecution? Biased in favor of the defense? Basically fair to both sides?

93. If you have discussed this case with friends and/or relatives, do your friends/relatives overall seem to lean toward thinking that O.J. Simpson is: Not guilty? Probably not guilty? Not sure? Probably guilty? Guilty?

94. This case will be closely followed by local, state, national and international electronic and print media. What is your reaction to this?

95. On average, how often have you talked with relatives or friends about this case? 5 to 10 times a day? 1 to 5 times a day? Once every other day or so? A couple of times a week? Once a week? Once a month? Almost never? Never?

96. Have you ever watched any television shows besides the news which had stories regarding this case? Yes? No? If yes, please explain which show(s) and what you recall about them.

97. Have you listened to radio talk shows about the case? Yes? No? If yes, please explain which show(s) and what you recall about them.

98. Have you read any of the polls concerning the public views of the likely outcome of the case? Yes? No? If yes, please describe what you recall.

99. Please describe your reaction to what you have read in the public opinion polls concerning the likely outcome of this case.

100. Did you write a letter to the defense, prosecution, police or judge about this case? Yes? No? If yes, please explain.

101. Did you call the police, the judge, or either the defense or the prosecution "800" hotline number regarding this case? Yes? No? If yes, please explain.

102. Do you have a relative, spouse, significant other, or close friend who wrote or called the police, the judge, or either the defense or prosecution "800" hotline number regarding this case? Yes? No? If yes, please explain.

103. What do you think about jurors appearing on talk shows after serving on a criminal trial jury?

104. Have you watched a juror or jurors in a particular case talk on television about their experience on the jury? Yes? No? If yes, what do you recall and what was your impression of his/her experience?

105. Have you listened on the radio to a juror or jurors in a particular case talk about their experience on the jury? Yes? No? If yes, what do you recall and what was your impression of his/her experience?

106. Have you read about a juror's experience on a particular case in a newspaper or magazine? Yes? No? If yes, what do you recall and what was your impression of his/her experience?

107. What do you think about a juror writing a book about his/her experience on a case?

108. Have you read any books or articles about a juror's experience on a jury? Yes? No? If yes, please explain.

109. If, as a juror on this case, you heard evidence that was in conflict with information you learned from the media, how would you resolve the conflict? Please explain.

110. Based on what you know of this case thus far, what are your views concerning the LAPD?

111. Have you followed any criminal cases in the media in the last 5 years? (e.g. Menendez, Damian Williams (Reginald Denny Beating Case), Rodney King, etc.) Yes? No? If yes, please list them and explain your impressions of each case.

X. FAMILIARITY WITH BRENTWOOD AREA OF LOS ANGELES

112. Have you ever worked or lived in the Brentwood area? Yes? No? If yes, please give the closest major cross-streets of the location, whether you lived or worked there and during what dates.

113. Have you ever had occasion to regularly drive through the Brentwood area? Yes? No? If yes, please explain the circumstances.

114. Have you visited the location of 875 So. Bundy since the date of the killings of Nicole Brown Simpson and Ronald Goldman? Yes? No? If yes, how many times have you gone there? Please describe your reason(s) for going there.

115. Have you ever visited the location of 360 Rockingham since the date of the killings of Nicole Brown Simpson and Ronald Goldman? Yes? No? If yes, please state how many times. Please describe your reason(s) for going there.

XI. FAMILIARITY WITH JUDGE—ATTORNEYS—PARTIES—VICTIMS—WITNESSES

116. Do you know personally, or are you personally acquainted with, judge or any members of the court staff? Hon. Lance A. Ito, Judge? Court clerk Deirdre Robertson? Court reporters Janet Moxham or Christine Olson? Bailiff—Deputy Sheriff Guy Magnera? None of the above?

117. Do you know ANY lawyers, judges, court clerks, court reporters, or bailiffs? Yes? No? If yes, what are their names and please describe how you know them.

118. Were you or anyone known to you acquainted with Ronald L. Goldman? Yes? No? If yes, please explain how:

119. Are you or anyone known to you acquainted with a member of Ronald L. Goldman's family? Yes? No? If yes, please explain how:

120. What is your impression of Ronald L. Goldman based upon what has been reported or published in the news media?

121. Were you or anyone known to you acquainted with Nicole Brown Simpson? Yes? No? If yes, please explain how:

122. Are you or anyone known to you acquainted with any member of Nicole Brown Simpson's family? Yes? No? If yes, please explain:

123. What is your impression of Nicole Brown Simpson based upon what has been reported or published in the news media?

124. Have you ever been to or seen Nicole Brown Simpson's residence at 875 South Bundy or at 325 Gretna Green in Los Angeles? Yes? No? If yes, please explain the circumstances:

125. Do you know or have you ever met:

    Robert Shapiro? Yes? No?

    Johnny Cochran? Yes? No?

Howard Weitzman? Yes? No?

Gerald Uelman? Yes? No?

F. Lee Bailey? Yes? No?

Alan Dershowitz? Yes? No?

Barry Scheck? Yes? No?

Skip Taft? Yes? No?

Robert Kardashian? Yes? No?

Sara Caplan? Yes? No?

Carl Douglas? Yes? No?

Karen Filippi? Yes? No?

Marcia Clark? Yes? No?

William Hodgman? Yes? No?

If yes, please explain:

126. Do you know any lawyers who practice criminal law, whether as defense attorneys or prosecutors? Yes? No? If so, please indicate whom you know and the nature of your contact with them.

127. What is your opinion, if any, about prosecuting attorneys in general?

128. What are your opinions, if any, about criminal defense attorneys in general?

129. Do you know any lawyers who do not practice criminal law? Yes? No? If so, please indicate whom you know and the nature of your contact with them.

130. Do you personally know anyone who works for:

Los Angeles District Attorney's Office? Yes? No?

Los Angeles City Attorney's Office? Yes? No?

Los Angeles Police Department? Yes? No?

Los Angeles Sheriff's Department? Yes? No?

Los Angeles Coroner's Office? Yes? No?

United States Attorney's Office? Yes? No?

Los Angeles County Probation Dept.? Yes? No?

FBI? Yes? No?

Any other federal, state or local police or law enforcement agency? Yes? No?

Any Public Defender's Office? Yes? No?

Please explain any "yes" answers:

XII. FAMILIARITY WITH THE DEFENDANT, O.J. SIMPSON

131. What was your first reaction to hearing that O.J. Simpson was a suspect in this case?

132. Have you ever met O.J. Simpson? Yes? No? If yes, please explain the circumstances:

133. Have you ever seen O.J. Simpson in person? Yes? No? If yes, please explain the circumstances:

134. Have you ever seen O.J. Simpson in any form of advertising, such as television commercials for Hertz Corp. or in orange juice advertisements? Yes? No?

    If yes, please describe what kind of advertising it was and what you recall about it:

    If yes, describe the image that O.J. Simpson seemed to portray in your opinion:

135. Did you see O.J. Simpson play football in college or as a professional football player? Yes? No? If yes, describe the circumstances and your feelings toward O.J. Simpson as a football player:

136. Have you seen O.J. Simpson on television as a football commentator? Yes? No? If yes, describe your feelings about O.J. Simpson based upon your observations of him as a commentator:

137. Have you seen O.J. Simpson as he appeared in movies such as *Roots* or *Naked Gun 2*? Yes? No? If yes, describe your feelings toward O.J. Simpson based upon your observations of him as an actor:

138. Based upon your feelings toward O.J. Simpson, are you inclined to believe him guilty of the crimes with which he has been charged? Yes? No? Please explain:

139. Based upon your feelings toward O.J. Simpson, are you inclined to believe him not guilty of the crimes with which he has been charged? Yes? No? Please explain:

140. What best describes your opinion of O.J. Simpson at this time? Positive? Negative? Neutral? Please explain:

141. Have you been to or seen O.J. Simpson's residence located at 360 N. Rockingham in Brentwood? Yes? No? Please explain:

142. Have you ever had any personal interaction with a celebrity (such as writing a celebrity a letter, receiving a letter or photograph from a

celebrity, or getting an autograph from a celebrity)? Yes? No? If yes, please explain:

143. Have you ever asked a celebrity for an autograph? Yes? No? If yes, whom did you ask:

144. Have you ever written to a celebrity? Yes? No? If yes, whom did you write:

145. Please name the person for whom you are a great fan and describe why you are a fan of that person.

146. Will you hold the prosecution to a higher standard than is legally required because the defendant is:

    African-American? Yes? No?

    Wealthy? Yes? No?

    Famous? Yes? No?

147. Does the fact that O.J. Simpson excelled at football make it unlikely in your mind that he could commit murder? Why or why not?

148. Do you feel you know O.J. Simpson because of his background and fame? Yes? No? Please explain:

149. Do you think you may find it more difficult to believe the evidence presented to you if it conflicts with your beliefs about O.J. Simpson?

    Why or why not?

150. Do you think O.J. Simpson's celebrity status may make it very difficult for you to find him guilty or not guilty regardless of what the evidence shows? Possibly? Probably? Probably not? Definitely not?

    Please explain.

151. Have you seen, heard or read any portion of the freeway pursuit of O.J. Simpson and Al Cowlings? Yes? No?

    A. If yes, approximately how many hours/minutes of the freeway pursuit did you watch on television or listen to on the radio?

    B. What did you think about the chase?

152. Did you go out to watch any portion of the pursuit? Yes? No?

    If yes, please state what you observed, where you observed it, when and for how long:

153. Have you seen, read, or heard any portion of the 911 calls made by Nicole Brown? Yes? No?

    If yes, what did you think about the calls?

154. Have you seen, read, or heard any information regarding the 1989 incident between Nicole Brown and O.J. Simpson? Yes? No?

    A. If yes, what did you think about the incident?

    B. If yes, how did you think it was handled by the court?

155. As a result of what you have seen or heard or read about this case, do you think O.J. Simpson is: Not guilty? More likely not guilty than guilty? More likely guilty than not guilty? Guilty? No opinion?

156. Have you purchased, or otherwise obtained, any commercial item relating to this case? (For example, a/the shirt, book, video or trading card) Yes? No?

    If yes, please describe the item(s) and what was depicted on the items(s).

157. Have you read any books and/or magazines about O.J. Simpson? Yes? No? If yes, please describe:

158. Have you or has anyone you know made a financial contribution to any organization supporting the defense or relatives of the victims in this case? Yes? No?

    If yes, please explain to whom you made the contribution and why:

159. After you learned that the defendant was charged with the murders of Ronald Goldman and Nicole Brown Simpson did your feelings about him change? Yes? No?

    Please explain your answer.

160. Do you have any affiliation of any kind with the University of Southern California? Yes? No?

    If yes, please explain:

161. Do you have any affiliation of any kind with professional sports? Yes? No?

    If yes, please explain:

XIII. DOMESTIC VIOLENCE—USE OF FORCE

162. Have you ever experienced domestic violence in your home, either growing up or as an adult? Yes? No?

    Please describe the circumstances and what impact it has had on you:

163. Have you ever had a relative or close friend experience domestic violence? Yes? No?

    If yes, please explain the circumstances and what effect it has had on you:

164. Have you or has someone you know had any contact with a family violence program, a battered women's shelter, or attended any programs concerning family or domestic violence? Yes? No?

    If yes, who was involved?

    Please explain the circumstances:

165. Have you ever had your spouse or significant other call police on you for any reason, even if you were not arrested? Yes? No?

    If yes, please explain the circumstances:

166. Have you ever called the police on your spouse or significant other for any reason, even if s-he was not arrested? Yes? No?

    If yes, please explain the circumstances:

167. Have you ever known anyone who had problems leaving an abusive relationship? Yes? No?

    If yes, who was involved?

    Please explain the circumstances:

168. Why do you think s-he had problems leaving the relationship?

169. Do you think that family violence is a family situation which should be handled entirely within the family? Yes? No?

    Please explain your answer regardless of whether you answered yes or no:

170. When is violence an appropriate response to domestic trouble?

171. Have you ever felt sufficiently frustrated within a domestic relationship that you considered violence?

172. Do you think using physical force on a fellow family member is sometimes justified?

    Please explain:

173. Do you think that violence that occurs in the home or between adult intimates should be looked at differently than violence that occurs between strangers?

174. Have you ever made any financial contributions to battered women's shelters or similar programs? Yes? No?

175. Do you believe people with professional lives that involve physical confrontation or the use of violence are more susceptible to imposing violent solutions in their personal lives? Yes? No?

    Please explain your answer:

176. What do you think is the main cause of domestic violence?

177. What kinds of things do you believe can cause a normally law-abiding person to commit acts of violence?

178. Do you believe violence between family or friends is more likely or less likely than between strangers: More likely? Less likely?

    Please explain your answer:

179. Have you ever had occasion to use a knife against another person (whether cutting or just brandishing), including in self defense? Yes? No?

    If yes, please explain:

180. "Male professional athletes who participate in contact sports are more aggressive in their personal lives than other people."

    Strongly agree? Agree? No opinion? Disagree? Strongly disagree?

181. "Male professional athletes who participate in contact sports are more aggressive towards women."

    Strongly agree? Agree? Disagree? Strongly disagree? No opinion?

XIV. ETHNIC PREJUDICE

182. How big a problem do you think racial discrimination against African-Americans is in Southern California?

    A very serious problem? A somewhat serious problem? Not too serious? Not at all serious? Not a problem?

183. Have you ever experienced fear of a person of another race? Yes? No?

    If yes, please explain the circumstances:

184. How do you feel about interracial marriages?

185. How would you feel if a close family member or relative married someone of a different race?

    Would favor it? Would not oppose it? Would oppose it?

    Please explain:

186. Have you ever dated a person of a different race? Yes? No? If yes, how did you feel about it?

187. Have you ever been exposed to persons who exhibited racial, sexual, religious and/or ethnic prejudice? Yes? No?

    If yes, please describe the experience:

    Would this experience in any way affect your ability to serve as a fair juror in this case? Why or why not?

188. "Some races and/or ethnic groups tend to be more violent than others."

     Strongly agree? Agree? Disagree? Strongly disagree? No opinion?

     If you wish to do so, please explain your answer:

189. Are you a member of any group or organization which is concerned with racial issues? Yes? No?

     If yes, please identify the groups:

190. Are you a member of any private club, civic, professional or fraternal organization which limits its membership on the basis of race, ethnic origin, gender or religion? Yes? No?

     If yes, please identify the group or organizations:

191. When you were growing up, what was the racial and ethnic make-up of your neighborhood?

192. Is there any racial or ethnic group that you do not feel comfortable being around? Yes? No?

     If yes, please explain:

XV. DNA

The ability of DNA analysis to prove the identity of the person(s) whose blood or hair is found at a crime scene has been the subject of some television and radio shows, and magazine and newspaper articles. The following questions pertain to this subject.

193. Before the Simpson case, did you read any book, articles, or magazines concerning DNA analysis? Yes? No?

     If yes, please name the book, magazine, newspaper or other periodical where you read about it and briefly describe what you recall having read.

194. Since the Simpson case, have you read any articles concerning DNA analysis? Yes? No?

     If yes, please indicate in which magazines or newspapers you read those articles and briefly describe what you recall having read.

195. Are you aware of any other court cases involving DNA analysis? Yes? No?

     If yes, please describe these cases as completely as possible and state what you recall about them and the role DNA analysis played in the outcome.

196. What is your view concerning the reliability of the DNA analysis to accurately identify a person as the possible source of blood or hair

found at a crime scene? Very reliable? Not very reliable? Somewhat reliable? Unreliable? Don't know?

Please explain your answer:

197. Have you followed any of the court hearings concerning DNA analysis in the Simpson case? Yes? No? If yes, please check all the media sources that apply:

> **Television:** Channel 2 News? Channel 4 News? Channel 5 News? Channel 7 News? Channel 9 News? Channel 11 News? Channel 13 News? Court TV? CNN? Other?
>
> **Radio:** KNX? KFI? KFWB?
>
> **Newspaper:** *L.A. Times? Daily News? USA Today? L.A. Sentinel?*
>
> **Magazine:** *Time? Newsweek? L.A. Magazine? People?* Other?
>
> **Tabloids:** *National Enquirer? Globe? Star? National Examiner?* Other?

198. From these sources, how much would you say you have heard about DNA analysis in the Simpson case?

     A lot? Some? Very little?

199. What do you recall hearing and/or reading about the DNA hearings in the Simpson case?

200. What are your views concerning what you have heard and/or read about the DNA hearings in the Simpson case?

XVI. RELIGION

201. A. Do you have a religious affiliation or preference? Yes? No?

     B. If yes, please describe:

     C. How important would you say religion is in your life?

     D. Would anything about your religious beliefs make it difficult for you to sit in judgment of another person? Yes? No? Possibly?

     E. How often do you attend religious services?

XVII. POLITICAL

202. What is your political affiliation? (please circle)

     1. Democrat

     2. Republican

     3. Independent

     4. Other (please specify)

203. Are you currently registered to vote? Yes? No?

204. Did you vote in the June, 1994 primary elections? Yes? No?

205. Do you consider yourself politically:

    Active? Moderately Active? Inactive?

XVIII. "EXPERT" WITNESSES

206. Have you ever consulted with an expert other than a medical doctor? Yes? No?

    If yes, please specify the type of expert and the purpose for which she was consulted.

207. When was the last time you contacted an expert, other than a medical doctor? How did you go about selecting the expert you contacted?

208. What factors would you use to determine whether an expert WAS qualified or not?

209. After consulting with the first expert, did you consult with another expert on the same subject? Yes? No?

210. Have you ever given a blood sample to your doctor for testing? Yes? No?

    If yes, have you ever felt uncomfortable with the accuracy of the results? Please explain:

211. Have you ever provided a urine sample to be analyzed for any purpose? Yes? No?

    If yes, did you feel comfortable with the accuracy of the results? Yes? No?

212. Do you believe it is immoral or wrong to do an amniocentesis to determine whether a fetus has a genetic defect? Yes? No? Don't have an opinion?

213. Have you or anyone close to you undergone an amniocentesis? Yes? No?

    If yes, were you confident in the accuracy of the results? Yes? No?

    If yes, please explain:

XIX. SCIENCE AND MATH COURSES

214. Do you have any specialized training in medicine, science or bio-logy? Yes? No?

    If yes, please describe:

215. Did you take science or math courses in college? Yes? No?

     If yes, please list them:

216. Please check the answer which best describes how comfortable you usually feel dealing with mathematical concepts:

     Usually very comfortable? Usually fairly comfortable? Usually fairly uncomfortable? Usually very uncomfortable?

217. Do you have any knowledge of the field of population genetics? Yes? No?

     If yes, please describe your understanding of this subject and how it relates to DNA analysis:

218. Have you ever taken any courses in population genetics? Yes? No?

     If so, please state when and where:

219. Have you ever taken any courses in statistics? Yes? No?

     If so, please state when and where:

220. Have you ever taken any courses in molecular biology? Yes? No?

     If so, please indicate when and where:

XX. VICTIM OR WITNESS TO CRIME

221. Are you or have you been a member of Neighborhood Watch? Yes? No? If yes, what was the nature of your involvement?

222. Do you have (please check)

     Security bars? Alarms? Guard dog? Weapons for self-protection?

223. Do you belong to any group or organization which is active in political matters or concerned with crime prevention or victims' rights? Yes? No?

     If yes, please describe:

224. Have you ever been a victim of a crime? Yes? No?

     If yes, how many times?

     What kind of crime(s)?

225. Did you or anyone else report it to the police? Yes? No?

     If no, why not?

226. Were you interviewed by police? Yes? No?

227. Was a suspect caught? Yes? No?

228. Do you feel the job the police did on it was:

     Satisfactory? Why?

     Unsatisfactory? Why?

229. Did you testify in court? Yes? No?

230. Have you ever seen a crime being committed (other than where you were the victim)?

    If yes, how many times and what kind of crime(s)?

231. Did you report it to the police? Yes? No?

    If no, why not?

232. Was a suspect caught? Yes? No?

233. Were you interviewed by police? Yes? No?

234. Did you testify in court? Yes? No?

XXI. CONTACTS WITH LAW ENFORCEMENT AGENCIES

235. Have you had a good or positive experience with any law enforcement agency, including the Los Angeles Police Department?

    Please explain and indicate the police agency involved:

236. Has any member of your family or any acquaintance had a good or positive experience with any law enforcement agency, including the Los Angeles Police Department?

    Please explain and indicate the police agency involved:

237. Have you had a bad or negative experience with any law enforcement agency, including the Los Angeles Police Department?

    Please explain and indicate the police agency involved:

238. Has any member of your family, or any acquaintance, had a bad or negative experience with any law enforcement agency, including the Los Angeles Police Department?

    Please explain and indicate the police agency involved:

XXII. CONTACTS WITH PROSECUTING AGENCIES

239. Have you had a good or positive experience with any prosecuting agency, including the Los Angeles County District Attorney's Office? Yes? No? If yes, please explain:

240. Have you had a bad or negative experience with any prosecuting agency, including Los Angeles County District Attorney's Office? Yes? No?

    If yes, please explain:

241. Have you or has any family member ever had occasion to use the services of the District Attorney's Office, for such services as the Family Support, Consumer Fraud, or Victim-Witness division? Yes? No?

If yes, please explain:

XXIII. CONTACT WITH CORONER'S OFFICE

242. Have you had a good or positive experience with any coroner's agency, including the Los Angeles Coroner's Office? Yes? No?

If yes, please explain:

243. Have you had a bad or negative experience with any coroner's agency, including the Los Angeles County Coroner's Office? Yes? No?

If yes, please explain:

XXIV. LEISURE ACTIVITIES—ENTERTAINMENT—HOBBIES—MISCELLANEOUS

244. What type of books do you prefer? (Example: Nonfiction? Historical? Romance? Espionage? Mystery?)

245. Do you read a newspaper on a regular basis? Yes? No?

If yes, which newspapers do you read on either a regular or occasional basis?

Los Angeles Times? Daily News? Los Angeles Sentinel? U.S.A. Today? Other? Please specify:

246. Which "news" magazines, if any, do you read on either a regular or occasional basis?

Time? Newsweek? People? The New Yorker? Los Angeles Magazine? Other? Please specify:

247. What magazines and newspapers, if any, do you subscribe to?

Time? Newsweek? People? The New Yorker? Los Angeles Magazine? Los Angeles Times? The Daily News? Los Angeles Sentinel? U.S. News and World Report? U.S.A. Today? Other? Please specify:

248. Have you ever written a letter to the editor of a newspaper or magazine? Yes? No?

If yes, what was the subject matter of your comment?

249. Which tabloids do you read on an occasional or regular basis?

> *The National Enquirer?* Occasionally? Regularly?
>
> *The Star?* Occasionally? Regularly?
>
> *The Globe?* Occasionally? Regularly?
>
> *The National Enquirer?* Occasionally? Regularly?
>
> Other? Please specify:

250. Which tabloids, if any, do you subscribe to?

> *The National Enquirer? The Star? The Globe? The National Enquirer?* Other? Please specify:

251. Which television news shows do you enjoy watching on a regular basis?

252. Do you ever watch TV programs that show real-life police activities such as *Cops, America's Most Wanted,* or *Unsolved Mysteries?* Yes? No?

> If yes, Very often? Occasionally? Almost never?

253. What is your most frequent source of news?

> Newspapers? TV? Radio? Magazines? Friends and family?

254. Which of the following programs do you watch on a regular basis? (Check all that apply.)

> Channel 2 Action News
>
> Noon? 5 p.m.? 6 p.m.? 11 p.m.?
>
> Channel 4 News
>
> Noon? 4 p.m.? 5 p.m.? 6 p.m.? 11 p.m.?
>
> Channel 7 News
>
> Noon? 5 p.m.? 6 p.m.? 11 p.m.?
>
> Local station (For example, Ch. 5, 9, 11, 13)

255. Do you watch any of the early news programs such as *Today, This Morning,* or *Good Morning America?* Yes? No?

> If yes, how often? (please check)
>
> Daily? Occasionally?

256. Do you watch any of the mid-morning "talk" shows, such as *Jenny Jones, Ricki Lake, Marilu,* etc.? Yes? No?

> If yes, how often? (please check) Daily? Occasionally?

257. Do you watch any of the afternoon "talk" shows, such as *Maury Povich, Donahue, Oprah, Sally Jessy Raphael,* etc.? Yes? No?

> If yes, how often? (please check)
>
> Daily? Occasionally?

— Do you watch any of the early evening "tabloid news" programs, such as *Hard Copy, Current Affair, American Journal*, etc.? Yes? No?

If yes, how often? (please check)

Daily? Occasionally?

258. Do you watch any of the prime-time news programs, such as *Primetime, 20-20, 60 Minutes, Dateline, 48 Hours*, etc.? Yes? No?

If yes, how often? (please check)

Daily? Occasionally?

259. Do you watch *Court TV*? Yes? No?

If yes, how often? (please check)

Daily? Occasionally?

260. What are your leisure time interests, hobbies and activities?

261. Do you like detective/crime drama movies, television programs or books? Yes? No?

If yes, please list the last 3 such movies, TV programs or books seen or read:

262. What accomplishments in your life are you most proud of?

263. What groups or organizations do you belong to now or have you belonged to for a significant period of time in the past? (For example, bowling leagues, church groups, AA, Sierra Club, MECLA, National Rifle Association, ACLU, YWCA, PTA, NAACP, etc.)

   A. Now:

   B. Previously:

   Have you served as an officer in any one of these groups? Yes? No?

   If yes, which group(s):

264. Do you currently, or have you during the past five years, done any volunteer work? If so, for what organization(s) is/was it?

265. Are there any charities or organizations to which you make donations? Yes? No?

   If yes, please list the organizations or charities to which you contribute:

266. Do you belong to or associate with any groups which have crime prevention or law enforcement as a primary goal? Yes? No?

   If yes, which groups?

XXV. SPORTS

267. What sports do you like to attend in person?

268. What sports do you like to watch on television?

269. Do you currently play any sport for recreation? Yes? No? If yes, which sport(s)?

270. Have you or any member of your family or friends ever played any college or professional sport? Yes? No? If yes, which sport(s) and for whom did you/they play?

271. Did you play any sport for fun growing up (other than for a school team)? Yes? No? If yes, which sport(s)?

272. Do you follow professional football? Yes? No?

273. Are you a fan of the USC Trojans football team? Yes? No? If yes, for how many years?

274. If not currently a fan, have you in the past ever been a fan of the USC Trojans football team? Yes? No? If yes, for how many years?

275. Are you or have you ever been a fan of the Buffalo Bills football team? Yes? No? If yes, for how many years? If yes, why are you or were you a fan of the Buffalo Bills?

276. During football season, do you watch football on television on the weekends? (Check the one answer that most applies:)

    ___ Every weekend without fail?

    ___ Almost every weekend?

    ___ Frequently?

    ___ Occasionally?

    ___ Seldom?

    ___ Almost never?

    ___ Never?

277. During football season, do you watch Monday night football? (Check the one answer which most applies:)

    ___ Every Monday night, without fail?

    ___ Almost every Monday night?

    ___ Frequently?

    ___ Occasionally?

    ___ Seldom?

    ___ Almost never?

    ___ Never?

278. How many hours per week do you watch sporting activities?

279. Name the last three sporting events you attended.

280. What are your favorite sports? Why?

281. Name the most significant sport figure, sport program, or sporting event scandals you recall.

282. Does playing sports build an individual's character? Yes? No? Please explain your answer whether you answer yes or no:

XXVI. DIVERSE

283. Do you seek out positions of leadership? (Please check answer:)

___ Always?

___ Often?

___ Seldom?

___ Never?

284. Please name the three public figures you admire most.

285. Do you think you might have difficulty judging someone who is charged with a crime? Yes? Probably yes? Probably not? No? Please explain your answer:

286. Do you think celebrities are held less responsible for their actions than the average person? Yes? No? Please explain your answer:

287. Do you believe people of wealth or fame are subject to the same personal problems as the common man or woman? Please explain:

288. Do you own any special knives (other than for cooking), such as for hunting or pen knives? Yes? No? If yes, please describe the knife or knives and your reasons for owning it or them:

289. Do you think crime is a serious problem in your city or area of Los Angeles? Yes? No? If yes, which of the following answers best reflects your view? The problem is very serious? The problem is somewhat serious? There is not a serious problem?

290. Have you ever been to a jail or prison for any reason? Yes? No? If yes, what was your purpose in going there?

XXVII. SITTING AS A JUROR ON THIS CASE

291. How do you feel about being a juror in this case? Please explain.

292. Would you like to be a juror in this case? Yes? No? Please explain.

293. Have you discussed with your family or friends the impact your service as a juror on this case may have? Yes? No? If yes, please explain. When did you have that discussion?

294. If you are selected as a juror in this case, how will your family handle and cope with the stress?

295. If you are selected as a juror in this case, considering all the media exposure on the case, will you be able to decide this case solely and entirely based upon the evidence presented to you during trial? Yes? No? Please explain your answer.

296. If you are selected as a juror in this case, will you base your decision on the defendant's guilt or innocence solely on the evidence presented to you during trial? Yes? No?

297. If you are selected as a juror in this case, will you set aside any personal feelings you may have about the defendant, positive or negative, and rely solely and exclusively on the evidence presented to you in court to decide this case? Yes? No? Please explain your answer.

298. If you are selected to serve as a juror on this case, would you be concerned about reactions to the verdict by:

    Friends? Yes? No?

    Relatives? Yes? No?

    The media? Yes? No?

    People in the community? Yes? No?

    If yes, what kind of concern(s) do you have? Please explain.

XXVIII. CONCLUDING QUESTIONS

299. As a result of filling out this questionnaire, have you now formed an opinion about this case? If yes, please explain.

300. Is there any matter not covered by this questionnaire that you think the attorneys or Court might want to know about you when considering you as a juror in this case?

301. Is there anything that has come to your attention since you first appeared in court on this case that would make your sitting as a juror on this case a financial or personal hardship? Yes? No? If yes, please explain.

GLOSSARY

Accessory: One who knowingly aids, but does not directly participate in, the commission of a crime.

Accessory after the fact: One who was not involved in the crime until after it was committed, but then assisted the perpetrator(s) in a material way.

Accomplice: Any one of the people actually involved in a crime that is committed by more than one person.

Aquittal: A jury verdict of "not guilty" in a criminal trial.

Admissible evidence: Testimony or physical evidence which the judge decides may be given to the **jury.**

Admission: A statement by the **defendant** that is considered damaging to his or her case, but is less than a **confession.**

Affidavit: A written statement sworn to before an officer of the court or a notary public.

Alibi: The statement by the **defendant** that he or she was elsewhere at the time of the crime, or a citation of other facts supposedly establishing his or her innocence. The term connotes neither belief nor disbelief in the statement.

Allegation: An assertion of a fact that one side or the other is going to attempt to prove.

Allen Charge: Named after *Allen v United States*, a Supreme Court decision allowing it. An Allen Charge is an instruction given by a judge to a **jury** in a criminal trial when the jury is having trouble reaching a decision. In essence, it tells a jury that it is the jury's responsibility to do everything possible to reach agreement, and that, although each juror must make an independent decision, giving due weight to the arguments of his or her fellows but not being intimidated by them, a holdout minority still might want to examine its opinion with care in view of the contrary opinion of the majority. There has been much criticism of the Allen Charge as being potentially unduly coercive, and its use has been modified in some jurisdictions.

Alternate juror: One who is selected as a juror beyond the necessary twelve, who is present in the jury box through the trial but is called upon to deliberate on the verdict only if one of the original twelve cannot serve.

Amicus Curiae: (Latin for "Friend of the Court") one who represents neither side of a case and who provides the court with information or specialized knowledge, usually in the form of a legal **brief.**

Appeal: A request for a higher court to review the decision of the trial court and find cause for a reversal of that decision or a new trial.

Appellate Court: A court with the authority to review the decisions of trial courts.

Arraignment: The process of formally charging a person with a crime and binding him or her over for trial.

Arrest: The placing of a person in custody to answer a specific criminal charge.

Arrest warrant: A warrant obtained from a judge based on probable cause to believe someone guilty of a crime. An arrest warrant permits police officers to enter someone's home to effect an arrest.

Attorney-client privilege: The absolute right, recognized in law, for both an attorney and his or her client to keep all communications between them confidential. This includes a client's discussion of having committed crimes, but does not permit privacy of discussion of future intended or pending crimes.

Bail: The posting or pledging of money or other valuables—usually real estate—to insure the presence of a **defendant** at all required proceedings.

Bench trial: A trial held by a judge without a **jury.** This practice, which has been acceptable in all states only within the past half-century, must be agreed to by both the defense and prosecution.

Bench warrant: A **warrant** issued by a judge to compel the presence of a person in court or elsewhere. Mostly used for witnesses who have failed to answer a subpoena or a charge of contempt of court, it permits the person named in the warrant to be apprehended by the police.

Beyond a reasonable doubt: The standard of belief that a **jury** must have in order to convict a **defendant** in a criminal trial.

Bill of Rights: The first ten amendments to the Constitution of the United States, which mostly enumerate specific rights, such as freedom of speech or religion (the First Amendment), or the right against self-incrimination (the Fifth Amendment), which are reserved to the people.

Bind over: To place a **defendant** in custody prior to trial. The **defendant** may then be released on **bail,** into someone's custody, or on his or her own recognizance (promise to appear for trial).

Brief: A document given to a judge by the attorneys on one side of a case that presents the arguments and precedents for points of law on which they want the judge to rule.

Burden of proof: In a criminal trial, the **defendant** is presumed to be innocent until found guilty by the **jury.** The prosecution must prove the defendant's guilt and therefore carries the burden of proof, as the defense doesn't have to prove anything.

Case Law: *See* **Common law.**

Certiorari: Latin for "to be informed." A Writ of *Certiorari* is the document used by a convicted **defendant** to request the appeals court to look at his or her case.

Chain of custody: The ability to verify the location of physical evidence continuously, from its collection to its appearance in court.

Challenge for cause: An attempt, which must be approved by the judge, by the prosecution or defense to remove a prospective juror for a specific reason that renders the juror ineligible to serve. Some reasons that might be accepted by a judge are a prejudice, a relationship with someone involved in the trial, or a relative who is a police officer or a trial attorney. *See* **Peremptory challenge.**

Change of venue: The moving of a trial from the county where the crime took place to another location, usually because of undue local publicity.

Charge: The specification of the criminal offense cited in an **indictment.** Also, the speech given to the **jury** by the judge at the end of a trial containing the legal instructions they are to follow while considering the case.

Circumstantial evidence: Indirect evidence from which a conclusion can be drawn.

Clear and convincing evidence: A standard of proof in between the preponderance of evidence, which is the standard required for a verdict in most civil trials, and beyond a reasonable doubt, which is the standard required for conviction in criminal trials. Some specific civil cases require this standard.

Closing statement: The summation made to the **jury** by each side at the end of the evidence phase of a trial.

Common law: That body of law based on precedent, that is, on the way similar cases were decided in the past, rather than on statute (laws passed by a legislative body).

Concurrent sentences: Sentences for two or more crimes that are to run at the same time, or are not **consecutive.**

Confession: A statement admitting guilt. If it is by the **defendant** in a criminal case, it must have been made voluntarily after a **Miranda warning** to be admissible at the trial.

Conflict of interest: A situation in which serving one client or cause might bring harm to another client or cause that one is also bound to serve.

Consecutive sentences: Sentences for two or more crimes that are to be served one after the other, where one sentence does not begin until another is completed. Opposite of **concurrent sentences.**

Contempt of court: An act which, in the opinion of the trial judge, serves to impair the dignity or effectiveness of the court or interferes with the orderly administration of justice. A person held in contempt of court can be fined or jailed at the discretion of the judge.

Conviction: In a criminal trial, a jury verdict of "guilty" on one or more counts with which a defendant is charged.

Cross-examination: Questioning of a witness after the direct examination by the attorney representing the other side. Cross-examination should be limited to questions about what was asked and answered during direct examination.

Curative instruction: An instruction by the judge to the jury to correct an error in testimony or procedure. An instruction to disregard testimony that has been struck from the record might be one such instruction.

Defendant: In criminal law, the person charged with the crime and who is being tried for it in a court of law.

Direct evidence: Evidence that is not **circumstantial.** The testimony of a police officer who apprehended the defendant during the commission of the crime would be direct evidence.

Direct examination: The examination of a witness by the advocate calling the witness to the stand. This is followed by **cross-examination** by the advocate for the opposing side.

Directed verdict: A verdict entered by the judge without giving the case to the **jury.** The judge might find, as a matter of law, that there is insufficient evidence to convict, for example. In a criminal case a directed verdict of not guilty is possible, but not one of guilty, as the defendant has an absolute right to a jury trial.

Discovery: The process prior to a trial by which one side is informed of the evidence and witnesses the other side plans to introduce. Long common in civil trials, discovery is now coming into use around the country in criminal trials.

District Attorney: The attorney paid by the state and representing the people, and whose responsibility is developing and prosecuting criminal cases.

Double jeopardy: The **Fifth Amendment** to the Constitution of the United States holds that no one can be "subject for the same offense to be put twice in jeopardy of life or limb." This prevents trying a person more than once for a criminal offense after "jeopardy has attached," which is when the **jury** has been sworn at the first trial or when the judge in a non-jury trial has heard the first piece of evidence. The exceptions to this are when a court of appeals grants a new trial after a conviction (a defendant found innocent cannot be retried), or when a mistrial has been declared due to manifest necessity.

Due process: The **Fifth Amendment** to the Constitution states that no person can "be deprived of life, liberty, or property, without due process of law." Originally merely a restriction on the federal government, the rule was extended to the states by the Fourteenth Amendment. In a criminal proceeding, this assures that the state and its representatives must follow the rule of law for a conviction to be valid.

Eighth Amendment: The Eighth Amendment to the Constitution of the United States, which prohibits—but does not define—cruel and unusual punishment. The Supreme Court has largely left it to the state courts to define in the matter of criminal sentences.

Evidence: Everything introduced to a **jury**, including testimony of witnesses and physical exhibits, for the purpose of determining the facts of the case and thus the guilt or innocence of the **defendant.**

Exclusionary rule: Based on a Supreme Court decision, the rule that otherwise acceptable evidence cannot be used in a trial if it was obtained by illegal police conduct, such as searching without immediate probable cause or a search warrant.

Exculpatory: A term describing **evidence** that tends to show the innocence or mitigate the guilt of a **defendant.**

Expert witness: A **witness** having particular knowledge about the subject on which he or she is to testify.

Felony: A major crime. The original Common Law felonies were arson, burglary, larceny, rape, robbery, mayhem, and murder.

Fifth Amendment: The Fifth Amendment to the Constitution of the United States, which guarantees that no person can be tried for a major crime unless he or she is first indicted by a **grand jury**. The **double jeopardy** protection and the right to **due process** are also in the amendment, as well as the provision that no one can be forced to testify against oneself.

Fourth Amendment: The Fourth Amendment to the Constitution of the United States, which protects against unreasonable search and seizure and requires that a **warrant** be issued by a magistrate upon demonstration of probable cause.

Fruit of the poisonous tree: The doctrine that states that if evidence is discovered in an illegal manner, say with an improper warrant, that evidence (the "tree") and any evidence developed from it (its "fruit") are inadmissible in court.

Frye Test: The basic test for the admission of evidence into the courtroom based on new scientific techniques. From a 1923 Court of Appeals decision, *Frye v The United States*, it states that the technique has to be generally accepted by experts in the field. It has since been modified several times, and the test in use varies from state to state. In the Federal Courts and some states, it has recently been supplanted by a test based on the Supreme Court decision in *Daubert v Merrell-Dow.*

Grand jury: The jury, usually of 23 people, that determines a crime has been committed and that there is reasonable cause to hold a specific person for trial before a **petit jury** for that crime. It does this by handing down an **indictment** drawn up for it by the district attorney.

Habeas corpus: Latin for "you have the body." The Writ of *Habeas Corpus,* also known as the Great Writ, of ancient and honorable lineage in British common law, is a request for a court to determine whether an individual in custody is being legally held. It is used to bring issues regarding the constitutionality of state criminal convictions before the federal judiciary. It is also the method of forcing the authorities to bring a prisoner before a judge and either charge that person with something or release him or her.

Hearsay: A type of evidence that is not normally admissible. When a **witness** on the stand quotes another person, this is hearsay evidence. Exceptions include dying declarations and official written statements.

Hung jury: A jury that cannot decide on a verdict. The trial so affected is declared a **mistrial.**

In camera: Latin for "in chambers." The term refers to proceedings held in the judge's chambers.

Indictment: A formal document charging someone with a crime and given to a grand jury for consideration. If the grand jury approves, the indictment is filed and the case can and must continue to trial.

Information: A written accusation signed by the district attorney charging someone with a crime. This is used by some states in place of or in addition to an **indictment.**

Jurisdiction: The authority of a court to hear and resolve a case.

Jury: A term that usually refers to the **petit jury,** the decider of facts at a trial. *See also* **Grand jury.**

Jury charge: The information regarding the law pertaining to a particular case given to the **jury** by the judge just before the jury deliberates.

Jury nullification: A **jury's** delivery of a "not guilty" verdict based on something other than the facts at issue. It could represent popular emotion, or may be intended to send a message regarding the perceived oppression of some minority group or that the jury felt the defendant was guilty of the offense charged but that the act was morally, although not legally, justified.

Leading question: A question to a **witness** that points to the answer wanted. This is improper on **direct examination,** but is allowed during **cross-examination.**

Malpractice: Improper, illegal, or immoral conduct of business by a professional, such as a doctor or lawyer.

Malum in se: (Latin for "evil in itself") An act that would be recognized as wrong in our society even without a specific law against it, such as murder or robbery.

Malum prohibitum: (Latin for "wrong because it is prohibited") An act that is wrong because there is a statute against it, such as driving without a license or, in many cities, smoking in a restaurant.

Mandatory sentence: A sentence that must be imposed for a certain crime, leaving no discretion to the court.

Miranda warning: Based on the **Fifth Amendment** right against self-incrimination, a ruling that anyone suspected of a crime must be warned that he or she has the right to remain silent and to have an attorney present at his/her questioning, and that anything the suspect says can be used against him or her in a court of law. The Supreme Court enunciated this in *Miranda v Arizona.*

Misdemeanor: A crime that is less serious than a **felony**, and for which a lesser sentence is imposed.

Mistrial: A trial that has been terminated before the finding of a verdict by the **jury**. The most common cause of mistrial is a deadlocked or **hung jury.**

Mitigating factors: Facts that tend to lessen the seriousness of an offense, and thus reduce the nature of the crime, as in designating a killing manslaughter rather than murder. Also includes facts about the crime or the defendant that might warrant a lesser sentence.

M'Naghten Rule: An early rule defining legal insanity.

Motion: An application to the court requesting a ruling.

Motion for a directed verdict: A request for the judge to find, as a matter of law, that there is insufficient **evidence** to find the **defendant** guilty of the charge, and therefore to find him or her innocent (guilt cannot be found by a directed verdict).

Motion to dismiss: A motion to set aside the trial for some procedural or factual reason. Dismissal without prejudice puts the case as it was before the trial and does not bar a retrial. Dismissal with prejudice bars a retrial on the same charges.

Motion to suppress evidence: A motion to bar the use of specific **evidence,** possibly because it was illegally obtained, or possibly because its use might be inflammatory.

Murder: The unlawful killing of a human being.

***Nolle prosequi*:** (Latin for "unwilling to prosecute") A formal declaration by the state's attorney that a case, or a specific part of a case, will no longer be prosecuted.

Objection: The means by which a trial attorney informs the judge that he or she believes that the question of the examining attorney, the response of the **witness**, or a specific bit of **evidence** should not be put before the jury.

Opening statement: The statement made by the prosecution and defense at the start of the trial (or, for the defense, at the start of the defense's case-in-chief). It tells the **jury** what the trial attorney hopes to prove, but is not **evidence.**

Own recognizance: In place of bail, a seemingly trustworthy defendant can be released on his or her "own recognizance"—a promise to return whenever required.

Parole: A release from prison with specific conditions that must be followed. A parolee who violates any of these conditions may be sent back to finish out his or her original sentence.

Penalty phase: The part of the trial during which a convicted **defendant** is sentenced. After a guilty **verdict** in a first-degree murder trial, if the prosecution is requesting the death penalty, the **jury** must decide based on a balance of "aggravating circumstances," which would favor the death penalty, and "mitigating circumstances," which would incline against it, whether capital punishment should be imposed.

Peremptory challenge: The removal of a prospective juror from the jury panel without a stated cause. In a criminal trial in most states, each side is given a specific number of peremptory challenges. *See* **Challenge for cause.**

Perjury: The act of knowingly making a false statement under oath.

Petit [petty] jury: The group of (usually) 12 people that decides on the facts at a trial and delivers a **verdict,** as opposed to a **grand jury.**

Plea bargain: An agreement between the prosecution and the defense whereby the **defendant** pleads guilty to a lesser offense and is assured of a lesser sentence, saving the prosecution the time-consuming and always chancy business of a trial.

Preliminary hearing: A hearing held to determine whether there is enough evidence to bind the suspect over until a **grand jury** can hand down an **indictment**.

Prima facie: (Latin for "on the face of it") Self-evident; not requiring further proof.

Privileged communications: Any conversation or other communication between an attorney and his or her client, doctor and patient, and several other special relationships, that is recognized by law as privileged and cannot be divulged.

Pro se: (Latin for "himself") Representing oneself in court without a lawyer.

Probable cause: Reasonably trustworthy information that a search and seizure or an arrest is warranted. In getting a search or arrest warrant, an officer must present an affidavit of such probable cause to the judge issuing the warrant. If the search or arrest is conducted without a warrant, the officer must be able to show such probable cause after the event, along with reasonable proof that there was no time or opportunity to get a warrant.

Probation: The suspending of a prison sentence subject to specific terms and conditions. If the conditions are not met, the probation can be revoked.

Prosecutor: The representative of the state who prepares and tries criminal cases.

Public defender: An attorney paid by the government to represent defendants who cannot afford to hire their own attorneys.

Reasonable doubt: The standard of proof required in criminal cases. "Beyond a reasonable doubt" does not signify an absolute certainty, which is nearly impossible to obtain, but it does indicate enough confidence in the conclusion to act upon it if it directly concerned you.

Right against self-incrimination: The right, guaranteed in the **Fifth Amendment** to the Constitution of the United States, of a person not to testify against him- or herself.

Search warrant: The warrant, issued by a judge on **probable cause,** for a specific location to be searched for specific objects or a specific class of objects.

Stare decisis: (Latin for "to stand by what has been decided") The common law principle that each case is to be decided, as closely as possible, on the basis of past decisions.

Subpoena: A writ compelling, by force of law, the appearance of a **witness** at a trial.

Summation: The closing argument to the **jury** of each side in a court action.

Testimony: Statements made at a trial by **witnesses** under oath.

Verdict: From the Latin *veritas dictum*, "to speak the truth," the finding of the **jury** (or judge if there is no jury) as to the truth of the charges against the **defendant.**

Voir dire: (French for "to speak the truth") The examination of potential jurors. It also can refer to a hearing held out of the **jury's** presence to decide whether certain evidence is admissible.

Warrant: A writ from a court permitting a specified act. *See* **Arrest warrant; Search warrant.**

Witness: A person who gives sworn **testimony** in a court case.

Writ: A document issued by a court to permit or compel a certain action within the authority of the court.

BIBLIOGRAPHY

Books marked with an asterisk (*) are either particularly well written or particularly useful in one or more aspects of this subject or both.

Abrahamsen, David, M.D. *The Mind of the Accused.* New York: Simon and Schuster, 1983.

*Alderman, Ellen, and Caroline Kennedy. *In Our Defense: The Bill of Rights In Action.* New York: Avon Books, 1991.

Amnesty International. *United States of America: The Death Penalty.* London: Amnesty International Publications, 1987.

*Bailey, F. Lee. *To Be a Trial Lawyer.* New York: John Wiley & Sons, 1994.

*Belli, Melvin M. *Ready for the Plaintiff.* New York: Bobbs-Merrill, 1956.

Bertsch, Steve. *Crisis in Our Courts.* Grand Rapids, Michigan: Gollehon Books, 1993.

Blackstone, William. *Commentaries on the Laws of England.* Oxford: 1765.

Bloomstein, Morris J. *Verdict: The Jury System.* New York: Dodd, Mead, 1972.

Branham, Vernon C., and Samuel B. Kutash, eds. *Encyclopedia of Criminology*. New York: Philosophical Library, 1949.

Browning, Frank, and John Gerassi. *The American Way of Crime*. New York: G. P. Putnam's Sons, 1980.

Caplan, Lincoln. *The Insanity Defense*. Boston: David R. Godine, 1984.

Dershowitz, Alan M. *The Best Defense*. New York: Random House, 1982.

*———. *Reversal of Fortune*. New York: Random House, 1986.

Fowler, Gene. *The Great Mouthpiece*. New York: Covici, Friede, Inc., 1931.

Frankfurter, Felix. *The Case of Sacco and Vanzetti*. Boston: Little, Brown and Company, 1927.

*Friedman, Lawrence M. *A History of American Law*. New York: Little Brown & Co. 1973, 1985.

*———. *Crime and Punishment in American History*. New York: Basic Books, 1993.

Fuller, Lon L. *Anatomy of the Law*. Reprint. Westport, CT: Greenwood Press, [1968] 1976.

Gilmore, Grant. *The Ages of American Law*. New Haven: Yale University Press, 1977.

*Higdon, Hal. *The Crime of the Century: The Leopold and Loeb Case*. New York: Putnam's, 1975.

Hinckeldey, Christoph, ed. *Criminal Justice Through the Ages*. Rothenburg, Germany: Mittelalterliches Kriminalmuseum, 1981.

Holmes, Paul. *The Sheppard Murder Case*. New York: David McKay Co., 1961.

Kempin, Frederick G., Jr. *Legal History: Law and Social Change*. New Jersey: Prentice-Hall, Inc., 1959.

*Knappman, Edward W., ed. *Great American Trials*. Detroit: Visible Ink Press, 1994.

Kolanda, Jo, and Judge Patricia Curley. *Trial By Jury*. New York: Franklin Watts, 1988.

*Kurland, Michael. *A Gallery of Rogues: Portraits in True Crime*. New York: Prentice Hall, 1994.

*———. *How To Solve a Murder: The Forensic Handbook*. New York: Macmillan, 1995.

*Levy, Leonard W. *Origins of the Fifth Amendment*. New York: Macmillan, 1986.

Loewy, Arnold H. *Criminal Law in a Nutshell*. St. Paul, MN: West Publishing Co., 1975.

*Loftus, Dr. Elizabeth, and Katherine Ketcham. *The Myth of Repressed Memory*. New York: St. Martin's Press, 1994.

*———. *Witness for the Defense*. New York: St. Martin's Press, 1991.

*Macdonald, John D. *No Deadly Drug*. New York: Doubleday, 1968.

Miller, Arthur R. *Miller's Court*. New York: Houghton Mifflin Co., 1982.

*Nizer, Louis. *My Life in Court*. New York: Doubleday & Co., 1961.

*———. *The Jury Returns*. New York: Doubleday & Co., 1966.

Palmer, Stuart. *The Psychology of Murder*. New York: Crowell, 1960 (also published as A Study of Murder).

Pfeffer, Leo. *This Honorable Court: A History of the United States Supreme Court*. Boston: Beacon Press, 1965.

Radelet, Michael L., Hugo Adam Bedau, and Constance E. Putnam. *In Spite of Innocence*. Boston: Northeastern University Press, 1992.

Schiller, Lawrence, and James Willwerth. *American Tragedy: The Uncensored Story of the Simpson Defense.* New York: Random House, 1996.

Shapiro, Martin. *Courts.* Chicago: The University of Chicago Press, 1981.

Stewart, James B. *The Prosecutors.* New York: Simon & Schuster, 1987.

*Stone, Irving. *Clarence Darrow for the Defense.* New York: Doubleday, 1941.

*Train, Arthur. *Courts and Criminals.* New York: Charles Scribner's Sons, 1926.

*————. *The Prisoner at the Bar.* New York: Charles Scribner's Sons, 1926.

*————. *True Stories of Crime.* New York: Charles Scribner's Sons, 1908.

Walker, Peter N. *The Courts of Law: A Guide to Their History and Working.* Newton Abbot, Devon, Great Britain: David and Charles, 1970.

*Walker, Stanley. *Mrs. Astor's Horse.* New York: Frederick A. Stokes Company, 1935.

*Wellman, Francis L. *The Art of Cross-Examination.* New York: Macmillan, 1931. [reprint Barnes & Noble, 1992]

Westlaw. *Washington Court Rules: 1993.* Saint Paul: West Publishing Co., 1992.

Wormser, Rene A. *The Story of the Law.* New York: Simon & Schuster, 1962.

INDEX